Jazz

100 ESSENTIAL CDs | THE ROUGH GUIDE

There are more than on~~~~~~~~~~~~~~~~~~~~~~
travel, phrasebook, and ~~~~~~~~~~~~~ destinations
from Amsterdam to Zimbabwe, languages from Czech to
Vietnamese, and musics from World to Opera and Jazz

Other 100 Essential CD titles

Blues • Classical • Opera
Reggae • Rock • Soul • Country

Rough Guides on the Internet

www.roughguides.com

Rough Guide Credits

Text editor: Orla Duane
Series editor: Mark Ellingham
Typesetting: Mike Hancock

Publishing Information

This first edition published July 2001 by
Rough Guides Ltd, 62–70 Shorts Gardens, London WC2H 9AH

Distributed by the Penguin Group:

Penguin Books Ltd, 27 Wrights Lane, London W8 5TZ
Penguin Putnam, Inc., 375 Hudson Street, New York 10014, USA
Penguin Books Australia Ltd, 487 Maroondah Highway,
PO Box 257, Ringwood, Victoria 3134, Australia
Penguin Books Canada Ltd, 10 Alcorn Avenue,
Toronto, Ontario, Canada M4V 1E4
Penguin Books (NZ) Ltd, 182–190 Wairau Road,
Auckland 10, New Zealand

Typeset in Bembo and Helvetica to an original design by Henry Iles.
Printed in Spain by Graphy Cems.

A catalogue record for this book is available from the British Library.
ISBN 1-85828-732-4

Jazz

| 100 ESSENTIAL CDs | THE ROUGH GUIDE |

**by Digby Fairweather
and Brian Priestley**

ROUGH
GUIDES

Contents

Introduction

There are two ways of looking at the writing of this little book: either as a labour of love or a worthless exercise. Unfortunately, the two terms are often interchangeable, making things doubly hard for the beleaguered authors. But there are points that require making.

Firstly, many great jazz artists – Armstrong, Ellington and Miles Davis, for only three random examples – could easily warrant a couple of dozen CDs each. All we can do is point you, the reader, towards one ineluctable essential (or, in a handful of cases, two or three) and then wish you good hunting in the future.

Secondly, we have been governed in our choices by what's currently available on CD, a situation as slippery as trying to hold an eel by the hand (and, indeed, illustrated by one deleted album being restored to the catalogue, apparently in response to inquiries from the authors). However, we are forced to disclaim responsibility for the absence of several acknowledged classics, and keep our eyes open for such discographic injustices to be amended in time for a later edition.

Thirdly, in the interests of economy, we have stuck to listing "single CDs" with only a couple of exceptions. But the ever-increasing plethora of fine (and often comparatively cheap) boxed collations of classic jazz titles are hard to overlook, nor should you overlook them, if finances permit, and they contain material we recommend (plus more).

Lastly, many major figures in jazz music – Teddy Wilson and Ben Webster, for two more examples – are listed here amongst "supporting cast" only. This is not because of any intentional downgrading of their central contribution to the music, just a lack of space. Even looking only at trumpeters, there are at least ten represented on other people's records who, in a larger book, would have their own entry. For instance, Chet Baker appears only with Gerry Mulligan, Don Cherry with Ornette Coleman and Carla Bley, and Clark Terry is on albums by Oscar Peterson and Thelonious Monk (now *there's* an interesting combination!).

Another group of artists should be mentioned – those players who don't make great albums under their own names, but are heard at their best working for other people. Compare this with the early days of jazz recording, when artists, who later would have doubtless received a long-term contract (Bix Beiderbecke or Charlie Christian), made most or all of their recordings as sidemen. Back then, we are also dealing not with albums conceived as such, but with anthologies, and, while for the biggest names there are several competing (and overlapping) releases, for some musicians there are too few suitable compilations.

The vast stylistic spread of jazz these days makes the reader's task slightly easier. It's unlikely that any one listener will want to acquire all 100 discs at once but, having found the names of artists who appeal most directly, it should now be easier to locate others in the same part of the spectrum. As with leafing through any alphabetic reference book, you can make unexpected discoveries and surprising connections that, over a period of time, will explain how jazz spread its tentacles like an octopus but has only one pair of eyes looking out at the world.

Acknowledgements

More than two pairs of ears made the choices in this book, and our thanks go to Ronald Atkins and John Corbett, who contributed descriptions of some favourite albums. We are also indebted to commissioning editor Jonathan Buckley and text editor Orla Duane, to Yvette Shea, whose supportiveness is never forgotten, and to Chris Parker. Several record companies helped by supplying current editions of the repertoire, and various reference books (not least *Jazz: The Rough Guide* by ourselves and Ian Carr) assisted in narrowing down the contents to a mere 100 CDs. Thanks are also due to Florence Halfon (Warner), Sharon Kelly (Sony), Bryan Koniarz (Verve), Trevor Manwaring (Harmonia Mundi), Gaylene Martin (Coalition), Neil Scaplehorn (Ace), Lotte Scheffner (Bielefelder Katalog), and Sian Williams and Steve Sanderson (New Note).

Digby Fairweather and Brian Priestley

Cannonball Adderley

Them Dirty Blues

Capitol, 2000 (rec. 1960)

Adderley (alto-sax), Nat Adderley (clarinet), Bobby Timmons, Barry Harris (piano), Sam Jones (bass), Louis Hayes (drums).

The improvising and bandleading abilities of Cannonball Adderley were used in different ways during different phases of his career. Making his first impact on the scene in 1955, a few months after the death of Charlie Parker, he was readily accepted as an affirmation of Parker's musical values, but was also seen by some perceptive observers as incorporating the warmth and full-toned grace of earlier altoists such as Benny Carter and Johnny Hodges. Certainly, the blues connection via Hodges was something that Miles Davis valued highly when employing him from 1957 to 1959, yet the fact of performing alongside Miles, and especially John Coltrane, led to some of Cannon's more exploratory playing.

The latter side of his work came to fruition on the album *Somethin' Else* (one of Davis's very few post-Parker recordings as a sideman) and perhaps on *Quintet In Chicago*, which features Coltrane and the rhythm section of Miles's band. When Adderley formed a new quintet in late 1959, its approach was distinct both from the previous phase and from the slightly polite hard-bop of his earlier 1955–57 group (reissued on *Sophisticated Swing*) – despite both quintets including bassist Sam Jones and younger brother Nat Adderley. He now focused more intently on the blues and the gospel influence that turned hard-bop into "soul jazz", eventually leading to the crossover hit "Mercy, Mercy, Mercy" (based on a piano figure that pianist Joe Zawinul happened on while backing singer Esther Marrow).

Them Dirty Blues finds Cannonball stylistically halfway between his Davis period and his later successes. The cutely named title track, close in tempo to "Parker's Mood" but emotionally at a distance from it, shows him toying with some of Bird's phraseology and ending up with a more optimistic, almost tongue-in-cheek version of the slow blues. Similarly, Nat's tune **Work Song** is inappropriately light-hearted for the title, yet uses its rhythmic form and achieves something very 1960 with it. Two other remarkably catchy tunes add to the appeal of the programme, Bobby Timmons's **Dat Dere** – like "Work Song", this soon gained words by Oscar Brown Jr. – and Duke Pearson's **Jeannine**, also recorded in the same year by Donald Byrd, with the composer at the piano.

The relatively new band was already in a state of transition, with Timmons (who had been hired away from Art Blakey's Jazz Messengers) making the first of the two sessions and then reuniting with Blakey. Both he and his replacement, the under-sung Barry Harris, are devotees of Bud Powell but, while Harris plays straight down the line, Timmons's Rococo gospelized style was much more fashionable. The uncomplicated drive of Jones and Louis Hayes (who left Horace Silver to join) keeps the soloists on their toes, and the sometimes derivative Nat Adderley is at the top of his form. But clearly the most commanding player is Cannon, from his lavish but lyrical decoration on the standard ballad **Easy Living** to his humorous, strutting phraseology of the medium and fast-medium tunes.

Now available again after a long hiatus, this unpretentious album represents some of the best of Adderley. The reissue running order suffers slightly from grouping the output of each session together, but the alternative versions (first released on a Landmark CD) of "Dat Dere" and "Work Song" – the latter with Timmons rather than Harris, who is on the originally issued take – are saved for the end of the programme. The less-than-perfect sound, and ditto the pianos on both sessions, hardly detract from the joyous music.

❧ We almost chose **Somethin' Else**, Blue Note, 1999 [1958]

Henry "Red" Allen

World On A String

RCA Bluebird, 1991 (rec. 1957)

Allen (trumpet), J.C. Higginbotham (trombone), Buster Bailey (clarinet), Marty Napoleon (piano), Everett Barksdale (guitar), Lloyd Trotman (bass), Cozy Cole (drums).

Trumpeters who achieved prominence from the later 1920s onwards faced one universal challenge – the audible supremacy of Louis Armstrong. Since matching Armstrong's strength and creativity was an impossibility, the only option was to find a different approach. And, although numerous trumpeter/cornettists (from Harry James to Nat Gonella) reexpressed their admiration for Armstrong in individual terms later on, only a handful found viable alternatives – among them Bix Beiderbecke, Roy Eldridge (to a degree) and Henry "Red" Allen.

Allen, born in New Orleans and the son of a famous brass-bandleader, Henry Allen Senior, had already worked with King Oliver and Luis Russell when in September 1933, with Fletcher Henderson's orchestra, he reasserted his originality with one of two classic solos (the other was by composer Coleman Hawkins) on a harmonically challenging contemporary composition by Hawkins called "Queer Notions". During his definitive contribution – full of sidelong polyrhythmic phrasing, avant-garde whole-tone intervals and a sound which was veiled yet huge as a whale – Allen made it plain that Armstrong's musical bravura, operatic lyricism and heart-on-sleeve approach to improvisation was only one route home. And, despite a life of performance-recording which resembled Armstrong's in a desire both to entertain and communicate, Allen's on-record career continued regularly to illustrate the central jazz qualification of originality, until by 1965

– several jazz eras later – he could still be described (by the gifted contemporary trumpeter Don Ellis, in *Downbeat* magazine) as "the most avant-garde trumpet-player in New York!".

This late-on pronouncement (Allen died in 1967 when only 59) helps emphasize the fact that his stylistic development regularly revealed new and glorious zeniths from the mid-1950s on. Despite his crowd-pleasing appearances at noisy venues like New York's Metropole from 1954 (plus contemporary recordings in which his stylistic devices seemed to be used for identical purposes), Allen, by now, could present the listener with ravishing jazz creations which from 1962 (with the issue of a classic quartet collection *Mr. Allen* and its live follow-up *Feelin' Good* from 1965) fully re-established him, like Earl Hines, as a premier jazz voice from an older era.

The recordings on **World On A String** are definitive early examples of this new creative dawn. Other trumpet-playing contemporaries – Rex Stewart, for example – cunningly crafted aspects of their later styles from technical limitation. Allen, in contrast (and like Louis Armstrong), was at the peak of his technical powers at this period, and all of his stylistic inventions – baby-tiger growls, shrouded long-tones, breathy explorations of the trumpet's lowest register, drastic melodic and harmonic surprises, fidgety sub-clause phrasings and much more – are displayed here as pure decoration to a dark-brown sound that pours out as easily and luxuriously as coffee topped with whipped cream. So good are Allen's theme-statement and solo on **I Cover The Waterfront** that they once achieved the singular tribute of LP reissue (on a classic RCA collection) minus the rest of the track – no doubt to the fury of the ever-competitive Coleman Hawkins, once again Allen's partner here. Throughout these titles Hawkins sounds like an angry bested heavyweight shouting for crowd support. At the conclusion of Allen's wondrous outing on **Let Me Miss You Baby**, his opening crotchet-triplet solo-entry sounds exactly like a man exclaiming "No, no, no – listen to me!" But this was Allen's night and Hawkins can only gallop after him like an avenging angel.

⮑We almost chose **Ride Red Ride!,** ASV Living Era, 2000 [1930–1946]

Louis Armstrong

The 25 Greatest Hot Fives & Hot Sevens

ASV Living Era, 1995 (rec. 1926–28)

Louis Armstrong (cornet, trumpet, vocals), with groups including Johnny Dodds, Jimmy Strong (clarinet), Kid Ory, Fred Robinson (trombone), Johnny St. Cyr, Nancy Cara (banjo), Lil Armstrong, Earl Hines (piano), Pete Briggs (tuba), Baby Dodds (drums) et al

While some important recorded precedents already existed, the recordings of Louis Armstrong's Hot Five and Hot Seven from 1925 to 1928 are generally accepted as the first definitive examples of jazz music on record. This was due principally to the emergent genius of Armstrong himself, whose musical contributions to his first solo recordings instantly established him (in Wynton Marsalis' phrase) as the "Shakespeare of Jazz". Records by the Hot Five and Seven – which were recognized at the time as a turning point for the music – sold out in the shops more quickly than they could be pressed, and created a generation of Armstrong disciples, many of whose descendants today believe that this was the greatest jazz ever recorded.

At this period Armstrong was still an effervescent young performer who could play anything he wished on his cornet, and whose creative gifts shone as brightly as the sun. Consequently, his music throws every musical emotion at the listener with an overwhelming, unaccountable generosity of spirit. Later, by the early 1930s, the young cornettist-turned-trumpeter was audibly honing his craft to point up its inherent profundities, and the beginnings of this process are clearly audible as this collection progresses.

The Hot Fives and Sevens are a cornucopia of musical jewels from which the musical hunter may fill and refill his treasure sacks ad infinitum. This ASV collection rightly cherry-picks many of their greatest musical – and historic – moments, beginning in 1926 with Armstrong's **Heebie Jeebies** (for which, by general account, he invented scat-singing, after dropping the song-sheet), the test-piece **Cornet Chop Suey** and four more, including the less widely heard **Jazz Lips** by Lil Hardin, in which, halfway through, Armstrong's ecstatic technical ease almost blows his instrument out straight. It's worth comparing this track with the almost uncomfortably profound feelings the 25-year-old Armstrong displays on the blues **Skid-dat-de-dat** which, cannily placed in this collection, follows one track later. Then come six absolutely central titles by the (electrically recorded) Hot Seven, including the magnificent minor-key **Wild Man Blues** (clarinettist Johnny Dodds makes a comparably dramatic contribution); **Potato Head Blues**, with Armstrong's now-classic stop-chorus, and the poignant **Melancholy Blues** in which a crying half-chorus from trombonist Kid Ory seems to bemoan Armstrong's flyaway mastery. Six more tracks (all from the Hot Five) in 1927 follow, including the triumphant **Struttin' With Some Barbecue** (based on the major seventh) and the joyful **Once In A While**. By track eighteen, the collection has introduced his principal creative rival, pianist Earl Hines, for **Skip The Gutter** and **West End Blues**, considered by some to be Armstrong's greatest recording from the era. His opening cadenza has remained a challenging test piece for later performers. As a bonus there are four sublime tracks by his Savoy Ballroom Five (including the spellbinding **Beau Koo Jack** and almost menacing **Muggles**), which add sophisticated dimensions to the music via Armstrong's new relationship with saxophonist-arranger Don Redman and his own developing aesthetic sensibilities as a soloist. For a capper comes the unsurpassed Armstrong–Hines duo on King Oliver's poetically titled **Weather Bird** – a sparring match between two acknowledged champions in which natural competition brings forth music of unaccountable majesty.

> ⤴We almost chose **Louis Armstrong 1928–29, Classics**, 1991, but couldn't quite afford **The Complete Louis Armstrong Hot Fives And Sevens**, CBS, 2000 [1925–28]

Louis Armstrong

Louis Armstrong Plays W.C. Handy

Columbia Legacy, 1997 (rec. 1954)

Armstrong (trumpet, vocals), Trummy Young (trombone), Barney Bigard (clarinet), Billy Kyle (piano), Arvell Shaw (bass), Barrett Deems (drums), Velma Middleton (vocals).

By the mid-1950s every aspect of Louis Armstrong's craft – creative, aesthetic, technical – had fused into the unconquerable artistic supremacy which, for those in the know, qualified him as jazz's premier genius. Regularly refining his solos like any great composer, until they became (in Ruby Braff's words) "a complete and perfect thing; a jewel", Armstrong was equally capable of bringing his mature creativity to new situations and material, displaying the same fantastical imagination which had exploded with his Hot Five and Seven thirty years before. The difference, by this period, was that Armstrong's performance exhibited unparalleled physical and aesthetic control. The resulting degree of personal nuance within his music celebrated such a combination of bravura majesty, high emotion and personal subtleties that it remains simply inimitable. Indeed Armstrong's musical output at this peak period seems not to have come from a trumpet at all; it resembles much more a clarion call from some superhuman source – a Gabriel on earth.

Armstrong made many definitive records at this time, but **W.C. Handy** is conceivably his greatest ever. To begin with, he is heading his All Stars – an unparalleled five-piece team whose solo strengths were in no way compromised by the supportive musical respect for their leader that Armstrong required. Equally central to this collection is the strength and dignity of its material – compositions by (or copyrighted by) "The Father of the

Blues", W.C. Handy, whose songs and themes allow Armstrong to explore every corner of his personal emotional landscape, amid well-loved classic territory. Most of the music here – selected by the session's visionary producer, George Avakian – was fresh to Armstrong who, with his All Stars and Avakian, prepared the music while honouring work commitments, prior to recording it over three evenings, in Chicago, in 1954.

From Armstrong's opening statement on **St. Louis Blues**, it is plain that the music is to be of extraordinary quality. The musical routines around him are subtly but perfectly tailored and, amid the choreography, Armstrong's majesty married to Handy's creations regularly produces true magic. Among such countless moments come the near-operatic ambience of a seldom-heard ensemble verse to **Loveless Love**; the yearning poignancy of **Hesitating Blues**; and Armstrong's remorseless repeated return to high-note climaxes at the awesome conclusion of **Chantez-les-bas**, a lesser-known Handy composition proposed by Avakian, whose long-term creative input into this project deserves full attention and respect. The high emotion of the music, however, is regularly leavened by Armstrong's vocal humour-cum-showmanship, often prompted by his amiable vocal partner Velma Middleton, most notably on the uproarious **Long Gone**.

In 1986, through a combination of unavoidable production problems, Armstrong's *W.C. Handy* collection was re-released on CD minus George Avakian's well-judged music-editing from 1954. This inadvertent desecration of a jazz icon was only corrected by Avakian himself in 1996, after new master sources were located to produce this definitive new CD reissue, which is unquestionably the one to buy. Truly worthwhile bonuses after the eleven original tracks include Avakian's respectful interview with W.C. Handy, Armstrong's famous Alligator Story (recorded in studio), and, best of all, three substantial rehearsal takes providing invaluable illustrations both of his in-studio methods and the daunting strengths of his team even before the red light went on.

⮌We almost chose **Louis Armstrong: A Musical Autobiography**

Volumes 1–3, Jazz Unlimited, 1993 [1956–57]

Art Ensemble Of Chicago

Nice Guys

ECM, 1994 (rec. 1978)

Lester Bowie (trumpet, celeste, bass-drum), Joseph Jarman (saxophones, clarinet, flugelhorn, conch-shell, vibraphone, gongs, whistles, vocals), Roscoe Mitchell (saxophones, flute, piccolo, oboe, clarinet, gongs), Malachi Favors Maghostus (bass, percussion, melodica), Famoudou Don Moye (drums, bells, bike-horn, congas, timpani, marimba, etc.).

The Art Ensemble of Chicago was the flagship group of Chicago's post-free jazz union, the Association for the Advancement of Creative Musicians (AACM). Starting in the late 1960s, they spanned the globe spreading the AACM message: "Great Black Music – Ancient To The Future". Organizationally, that über-principle dealt with self-determination; musically, it was a matter of inclusivity. Where the free-jazz revolution had a purist streak, the AACM musicians turned history into their flea market, mixing and matching different materials, styles and ideas, integrating r&b, funk, gospel, bop, free, classical, using instruments from other cultures. Such innovation meant checking the rear-view mirror, and personalization entailed looking far afield to look within. As saxophonist Joseph Jarman put it: "You must make it your responsibility even to understand what Muzak is about and how it's constructed. All these sounds and silences, and all these instruments, are just tools."

The quintet brought their entire arsenal to bear on the 1978 classic **Nice Guys**, the best of several fine records on the ECM label (*Urban Bushmen* and *Full Force* are also excellent). Trumpeter Lester Bowie brought his playful attitude up to the Windy City from St. Louis, and his **Ja** opens the date with a stunning bit of polystylism. A lush, long-tone theme and busy percussion establish a pastoral mood, then one little cymbal ring, and the composition jump-cuts into a bouncy autobiographical ska-calypso shuffle, Bowie slurring and blatting magical trumpet fills. The title track is a sweet, circusy miniature by saxophonist Roscoe Mitchell that starts and stops with a cheeky vocal – "They're SO nice...!" – and a flourish of vaudevillian bicycle horns.

Mitchell's **CYP** is a pointillist timbral study; the multi-reed-man likes to contrast colours: sax-click-brass-click-conga-click-melodica-click-celeste. Drummer Don Moye contributes **Folkus**, a similarly open piece that features his "Sun Percussion" (a vastly augmented kit) and the so-called "little instruments" (tables of miscellaneous noisemakers, deployed at strategic moments) introduced by bassist Malachi Favors Maghostus. From a sparse opening, things grow more discordant, sprouting into all variety of whizz-bangs, bells, chimes and vibes. Finally, the track transmutes into an African drum choir with horns.

Jarman's two tracks are the CD's trump card. **597–59** is a great post-Dolphy, multi-thematic construction. Mitchell uncorks an extreme solo over fiery rhythm section, his alto-sax distending agonistically; later, the horns play soft unison support under Favors' inventive bass statement. **Dreaming Of The Master** became something of a set-ending theme for the Art Ensemble. It's the longest track, nearly twelve minutes, which allows Bowie to spread out his solo in a fascinating way, but the slinky, blues-based mid-tempo swing of the first part abruptly leaps into a devilishly fast potboiler, spurring Jarman to dig hard into a expressive free-jazz tenor solo, before the neat theme returns for a recap.

The Art Ensemble still nominally works as a trio – Jarman left the band some years back to pursue his studies in Buddhism and Lester Bowie died in 1999, much too young. Their best work, like that of Henry Threadgill, Muhal Richard Abrams, Fred Anderson, Wadada Leo Smith and George Lewis, shows definitively that free-jazz was not in any way a dead end, but rather an open invitation to create.

⊃We almost chose **Les Stances A Sophie**, Nessa/Universal

Sound, 2000 [1970]

Albert Ayler

Spiritual Unity

ESP/Get Back, 1999 (rec. 1964)

Ayler (tenor-sax), Gary Peacock (bass), Sonny Murray (drums).

In the middle of the 1960s, New York City's free-jazz underground was in full bloom, a ground-zero atmosphere of experimentation and innovation. The primary label documenting this burst of activity was ESP, a gritty outfit with the vanguardist motto: "You Never Heard Such Sounds In Your Life". Saxophonist Albert Ayler originally hailed from Cleveland, but he left an indelible mark on New York's "new thing", suggesting a startlingly fresh method for making collective improvised music. In 1964, Ayler recorded **Spiritual Unity**, the first LP of music released on ESP. It was the pinnacle of a tragically short career – in 1970, Ayler's body was discovered in the East River, his death an unsolved mystery.

Spiritual Unity is perhaps the most fully realized free-jazz record ever made, a model of group interaction at the most subtle, intricate and elusive level. Bare-bones trio – sax, bass, drums – allows a demonstration of free music's interrogation of instrumental roles: no comping chordalist, no bassist sketching out the harmony, no drummer charting the time, no solos in a standard song form. This is music on scorched earth, inventing its own rules and freely exchanging prescribed musical roles. Bassist Gary Peacock is inhuman here, extending the virtuosity of speed-demon Scott LaFaro into totally open terrain; Peacock's mercurial lines are every bit to the fore as Ayler's saxophone, his musicality a constant marvel. Bass and tenor swoop together organically, Peacock thwacking an open string then sprinting up into cello position, Ayler reaching for a guttural love cry and conjuring the most ferocious and passionate spirits yet heard from his horn.

On the record's two versions of Ayler's best-known composition, **Ghosts**, the saxophonist's power and significance are immediately apparent. Out of the catchy, Caribbean-sounding theme, he explodes in a blaze of splintered and overblown firespitting, updating the expressionist r&b of honkers and shouters like Big Jay McNeely, Illinois Jacquet and Joe Houston. It's high-impact action-jazz, but don't miss Ayler's gentle rocking trill at the end of the first version. Drummer Sonny Murray plays with incredible sensitivity on this record; one could, in fact, call him delicate much of the time. The miracle is that he can still deliver such incredible energy without cranking the decibels, a feat that very few of his acolytes have taken to heart. Murray used a tiny kit here – no thundering tom-toms, only a snappy snare and lots of shimmering cymbals. On the very first issue of the record he was listed only as playing "brushes". In truth, Murray also used sticks, but so lightly and buoyantly that it's not a ludicrous mistake. **The Wizard** is another burner, while **Spirits** shows another side of Ayler: his mournful, dirge-like ballads.

Spiritual Unity is one of the monumental cathartic experiences in jazz, a record that demands to be listened to in a single sitting, with full attention. If you do so, maybe you'll notice something that's never, to the best of our knowledge, been acknowledged in print. You see, there's an old story about this record, that the sound engineer was totally unprepared for these heretofore unheard sounds, and that when Ayler started playing he ran out of the studio in fear. Apocryphal? Of course. But if you listen very carefully, at 3:22 minutes into the final track, the second take of "Ghosts", you'll hear the engineer lay five seconds of test tone! Perhaps the dingbat thought they were still warming up. They were already very warm. And playing for keeps.

⊃We almost chose **Vibrations,** Freedom, 1992 [1964]

Count Basie

The Original American Decca Recordings

MCA/GRP, 1992 (rec. 1937–39)

Basie (piano), including Buck Clayton, Ed Lewis, Harry Edison (trumpet), Eddie Durham, Benny Morton, Dicky Wells (trombone), Earl Warren, Lester Young, Herschel Evans, Jack Washington (reeds), Freddie Green (guitar), Walter Page (bass), Jo Jones (drums).

Compared to some other famous orchestral leaders from the formative years of jazz (Paul Whiteman, Duke Ellington, Fletcher Henderson up to Benny Goodman), Count Basie's orchestra – which first attracted the attention of record producer John Hammond while broadcasting on experimental radio from Kansas City's Reno Club in late 1935 – was a looser, less-formalized cabal. One (possibly overstated) condemnation of the orchestra came from George T. Simon in *Metronome* magazine: "If you think that sax section is out of tune, then catch the brass! And if you think the brass by itself is out of tune, catch the intonation of the band as a whole!"

By January 1937, when that review was written, Basie had just begun recording for Hammond and Decca, leading a band which already included star soloists – trumpeter Buck Clayton and tandem tenor-saxophone rivals Lester Young and Herschel Evans, as well as singer "Little" Jimmy Rushing. By March that year Freddie Green had joined Walter Page, Jo Jones and Basie himself to complete the leader's famed All-American Rhythm Section. "To not swing with them behind you, you had to be dead," observed trumpeter Harry Edison later, and within eighteen months more cornermen were to join, including the orange-toned lead altoist Earl Warren, Edison, and Dickie Wells, whose irreverent trombone would become another central solo focus for the orchestra. Such a wealth of individual talent had welded itself into an efficient unit by now, and more regular broadcasting – this time for CBS from Willard Alexander's Famous Door on Broadway – finally secured Basie his first hit: **Jumpin' At The Woodside**, six months after it was first recorded, in December 1938.

The band had been recording for almost two years by then, and the 63 tracks of this three-CD chronology tell its full on-record story for the Decca label from January 1937 to February 1939. Count Basie and his Orchestra set their own terms of reference early on. Compared to, say, Benny Goodman's contemporaneous output, their music sounds both looser and more effortlessly swinging. And, although Basie's arrangements, as the start of this set shows, were simply conceived to begin with, the pace quickly picked up: within months his band would boast state-of-the-art classics such as Eddie Durham's **One O'Clock Jump**, **Topsy** and **Swingin' The Blues**; Andy Gibson's **Shorty George**, and many more. Only the occasional ensemble oddity (Dicky Wells' trombonistic whoop of joy at the coda of **Every Tub**, for example, or scattered ensemble *gaucheries* like Durham's final ensemble on **Out The Window**) reminds us that this is Basie's good-sounding band rather than the (admittedly admirable) regiments of Dorsey or Goodman.

Best of all, of course, are the soloists. Lester Young, Buck Clayton, Dicky Wells – and of course Basie, with his famously economical piano contributions – were to become premier individual voices in jazz, and their contributions make the records great. Lester Young's poised entry and inspired opening statement on "Every Tub" is still sensational 63 years after its recording. Harry Edison's crying, flailing solo which ends "Swingin' The Blues" follows the kind of enviable soloists' parade – comprising Benny Morton, Young, Clayton and Evans – which repeatedly emerged from the Basie ensemble. Jimmy Rushing's ingratiating plum-coloured vocals are invaluable bonuses on their own, but all of this is music to treasure.

⮌We almost chose **Count Basie: This Is Jazz**, Columbia, 1996 [1939–62]

Count Basie

The Complete Atomic Basie

Roulette, 1994 (rec. 1957)

Basie (piano, leader), Wendell Culley, Snooky Young, Thad Jones, Joe Newman (trumpets), Henry Coker, Al Grey, Benny Powell (trombones), Marshall Royal, Frank Wess, Eddie "Lockjaw" Davis, Frank Foster, Charlie Fowlkes (reeds), Freddie Green (guitar), Eddie Jones (bass), Sonny Payne (drums), Joe Williams (vocals).

When **The Complete Atomic Basie** was recorded in October 1957, Count Basie and his orchestra had survived at least three incarnations – golden beginnings (as above), less comfortable postwar years (when bebop was making musicians of the swing-era edgy and affecting their output accordingly), and a third period of true renaissance between 1952 and 1954, recording for Norman Granz's Verve label. It was at this point that Basie triumphantly re-affirmed his premier position as big-bandleader after three years reluctantly leading an octet, and he did it with a sixteen-piece orchestra boasting new soloists, among them trumpeters Joe Newman and Thad Jones, trombonist Henry Coker, and two new tandem-tenorists, Frank Foster and Frank Wess. In turn, two phenomenal arrangers crafted Basie's new sound – Neal Hefti and Ernie Wilkins, who played alto and tenor in his leader's saxophone section from 1952 to 1955. In this good company, along with sex-symbol singer Joe Williams (who joined him in 1954), Basie returned to on-record hitmaking including "Alright, OK, You Win!" and "Every Day I Have The Blues", as well as a popular instrumental classic of his own – the three-time finisher "April In Paris" – alongside a stylish string of Wilkins and Hefti creations.

When *The Complete Atomic Basie* was issued on Roulette, it caused new sensations for at least two reasons. The first was its highly controversial cover art, depicting a nuclear explosion. More to the point, with this album Basie conclusively demonstrated that his band was ahead of the game, boasting ensemble powers to surpass any of its predecessors (and probably rivals, too), plus the ability to outswing all of them for good measure. In the five years to come, Basie would record more fine albums (including *Chairman Of The Board* and Benny Carter's *Kansas City Suite*) but *The Complete Atomic Basie*, composed and arranged solely by Neal Hefti, is his last great public landmark, and the music it contains deserves its reputation.

Hefti chose to open his arranger's masterpiece, surprisingly, with a feature for (and titular dedication to) his leader, **The Kid From Red Bank** – a *tour de force* in which Basie's piano is featured first in skipping single-lines then erupting into galloping stride-piano while pursued relentlessly by his band. This remarkable re-establishment of the leader's Fats Waller-style gifts in a 1950s jazz-piano era more notable for cool understatement and "right-hand only" performance was a true track-one showstopper, and from there on everything else measured up, then, as it still does today. Trumpeters Joe Newman and Thad Jones team stylishly for **Duet**; altoist Frank Wess solos faultlessly (if only occasionally) but hero of the hour is Eddie "Lockjaw" Davis, whose baleful r&b inflected tenor regularly tears in on the ensemble as angrily as if he were chasing his leader for an overdue raise. Davis causes alarm but no despondency on Hefti masterpieces including **Flight Of The Foo Birds** and **Whirly Bird** (with its polyrhythmic finale depicting swirling helicopter-blades). And as its climax this great collection presented the gracefully measured **Lil' Darlin** – still a control test piece for big bands everywhere – featuring a rare but superbly lyrical solo from lead trumpeter Wendell Culley. For Culley, Basie and Davis *The Complete Atomic Basie* might stand proud as a communal epitaph; for Hefti it remains his masterpiece in jazz history. The CD offers five bonus tracks, probably all arranged by Jimmy Mundy, but sensibly they are placed after the Hefti explosion.

⟳We almost chose **April In Paris**, Verve, 2000 [1957]

Sidney Bechet

Really The Blues

ASV Living Era, 1993 (rec. 1932–41)

Bechet (soprano-sax, clarinet), with his New Orleans Feetwarmers, Trio, Tommy Ladnier, Jelly Roll Morton, Bechet-Spanier Big Four, Louis Armstrong, Dr. Henry Levine's Barefoot Dixioland Philharmonic.

In the history of jazz, Sidney Bechet's musical achievements are comparable to those of Louis Armstrong's but the comparison is seldom made between the two, and this, on the face of it, is rather surprising. By 1918 (when Armstrong was still in New Orleans), Bechet was already on the road to international acclaim with Will Marion Cook's Southern Syncopators. In a rare paean of praise from such musically elevated quarters, classical conductor Ernest Ansermet wrote of Bechet's London concert at the time: "Perhaps his way is the highway along which the whole world will swing tomorrow!"

History has proven, however, that Ansermet's prediction applied only to the jazz world. Bechet's achievements were mighty, but unlike Armstrong his talent is still less talked of than it should be, despite the fact that he is championed by premier contemporary figures such as one-time pupil Bob Wilber and trumpeter Humphrey Lyttelton. Possibly Bechet's career, though highly successful, was self-confined by his personality (he lacked both Armstrong's outward wish to please and accessible star quality) and for much of the time he played the soprano saxophone with a challengingly wide vibrato which, like his instrument itself, was not to everyone's taste. Indeed, despite his pupil Johnny Hodges' use of the soprano-sax early on, it was still only with the advent of John Coltrane in the 1960s, and subsequent impressionists like Wilber and Kenny Davern, that the soprano-sax gained widespread acceptance.

Undoubtedly, too, Bechet lacked Armstrong's final brush strokes of genius. But he was a jazz giant nevertheless and this ASV **Really The Blues** collection, compiled by Vic Bellerby and pianist Pat Hawes, is a wholly admirable portrait of Bechet's music. First come two unstoppable titles by his New Orleans Feetwarmers from 1932, opening with **Lay Your Racket** in which Bechet, typically, can't wait to play, unleashing his inspiration like an angry tiger throughout an opening ensemble and solo, and returning ever more fiercely after Billy Maxey's vocal. From here this chronological set covers nine years of Bechet's work in 25 tracks. High spots include two classics by Tommy Ladnier – **When You And I Were Young Maggie** and the immortal **Really The Blues** on which Bechet's semi-scored duet with regular colleague "Mezz" Mezzrow creates a jazz monument before he returns, after Ladnier, for two final passionate choruses (Bechet, like Coleman Hawkins, enjoyed having the last word).

Pairs of titles which follow include wonderful, rather formalized sides by Jelly Roll Morton's New Orleans Jazzmen; two of the best by the delicately balanced Bechet-Spanier Big Four from 1940 (with a great guitarist, Carmen Mastren, and Wellman Braud on bass), and two more indispensable recordings by Louis Armstrong and his Orchestra, which (as John Chilton has pointed out in his definitive biography of Bechet, *The Wizard Of Jazz* 1987) emerge triumphantly into jazz's discography despite controversial accounts of the session on the day. Bechet is wisely illustrated as soloist and adventurous repertorian with rhythm section only via **Indian Summer** from 1940 and **Strange Fruit** from 1941, teamed with the great Willie "The Lion" Smith. And later impeccable choices include dates with sidemen, including J.C. Higginbotham and Charlie Shavers. Standing supreme, however, is **Blues In Thirds**, with Earl Hines' chiming piano, Baby Dodds' discreet drums and Bechet's yearning clarinet; spellbinding music from jazz's wizard.

⊃No alternative – **nothing else is as comprehensive**

Bix Beiderbecke

At The Jazz Band Ball

ASV Living Era, 1991 (rec. 1924–30)

Beiderbecke (cornet), with Wolverines, Sioux City Six, Rhythm Jugglers, Frankie Trumbauer, Jean Goldkette Orchestra, Bix's Gang, Paul Whiteman Orchestra, Bix Beiderbecke Orchestra.

Cornettist Bix Beiderbecke was the first jazz musician to achieve authentic legendary status, and might, in different circumstances, have done it for purely musical reasons. At a time when Louis Armstrong was establishing new levels and standards for jazz improvisation, Beiderbecke – on the same instrument – presented radical and relevant alternatives to Armstrong's musical solutions. And his playing at the time, both on and off record was passionately admired, not least by Armstrong himself, who in 1954 said of his one-time contemporary: "Just that name alone will make one stand up – also their ears! And when he played – why, the ears did the same thing!"

Beiderbecke's story has been masterfully chronologized by author/cornettist Dick Sudhalter in his 1974 biography, *Bix: Man And Legend*, co-written with Philip R. Evans and William Dean Myatt. Sudhalter's account dismisses the aftertastes of a romantic novel inspired by Beiderbecke's music (*Young Man With A Horn*, written by Dorothy Baker in 1938 and subsequently turned into a 1950 Hollywood fantasy starring Kirk Douglas, as well as the inaccuracies of a previous spurious biography, *Bugles For Beiderbecke* (by Charles Wareing and George Garlick, 1958). He had plenty of misconceptions to correct, and his book – which is required reading – tells the story of a supremely gifted young cornettist/pianist driven to a premature death from lobar pneumonia at the age of 28 as a result of peer and performance pressures, alcoholism and personal frustrations.

Beiderbecke's career on record spans just six and three-quarter years (from January 1924, when he first recorded with the Wolverine Orchestra for Gennett until September 1930 and his last date with Hoagy Carmichael) but this brief period covers a great deal of varied and essential territory. Almost all the major stages of Beiderbecke's on-record career are represented on this excellent ASV collection, compiled by authority Vic Bellerby, beginning with two tracks by the Wolverines and moving on to significant studio dates by the Sioux City Six and then Bix and his Rhythm Jugglers, who recorded the important Beiderbecke composition **Davenport Blues**, included here. Then come six crafted and modernistic tracks by Frank Trumbauer's Orchestra which have long been definitive representations of Bix at his peak – notably the artfully voiced **Way Down Yonder In New Orleans**, the bell-toned **I'm Comin' Virginia**, the jaunty **Ostrich Walk** and his on-record masterpiece **Singin' The Blues**. From here the collection touches on Beiderbecke's significant tenure with Jean Goldkette's orchestra (**Clementine**) before turning to three of his best small-group "Gang" recordings, and from there bravely touching on his Whiteman period with three topnotch tracks – the headlong **San** arranged by Bill Challis with trumpet trio for Beiderbecke, Jimmy Dorsey and Charlie Margulis; and two more, **From Monday On**, featuring Paul Whiteman's Rhythm Boys with Bing Crosby, and **Mississippi Mud** (with the Rhythm Boys, Crosby and Irene Taylor). Perhaps wisely, the collection chooses to avoid Beiderbecke's halting last recordings with Hoagy Carmichael, preferring to close with one of three Bix-led sides from September 1930 plus the essential **For No Reason At All In C** with the trio of Beiderbecke (on piano and cornet), Trumbauer and Eddie Lang, and closing quietly with his visionary piano solo, **In A Mist**. A near-definitive single-CD portrait of jazz's legendary "Young man with a horn".

⮌We almost chose **The Complete Bix Beiderbecke In Chronological Order**, IRD Records, 1991

Art Blakey

The Jazz Messengers

Columbia, 1997 (rec. 1956)

Blakey (drums), Donald Byrd (trumpet), Hank Mobley (tenor-sax), Horace Silver (piano), Doug Watkins (bass).

One of the most invigorating sounds in all of jazz is a small group led from the drums by Blakey. That he filled this role continuously for 35 years, from the mid-1950s until shortly before his death in 1990, attests to a certain dedication and a desire to pass on his methods and his acquired wisdom to ever-younger band members. Just a few of those who benefited in this way before going on to individual fame are Clifford Brown, Lee Morgan, Wayne Shorter, Keith Jarrett, Chick Corea and Wynton Marsalis.

What they all gained from Blakey included, of course, their initial exposure on the US jazz scene. But they also learned how to lead fellow musicians, to mould them into a cohesive group and, perhaps even more importantly, how to involve and communicate with an audience. Hence the name "The Jazz Messengers", which Blakey first used in person and on record as early as 1947, between working with the likes of Billy Eckstine's star-studded band and with Charlie Parker. But, along with many players of the bebop generation, he didn't begin to break through to a wider public until around 1954, when he formed a "collective" band with pianist-composer Horace Silver, bassist Doug Watkins, saxist Hank Mobley and trumpeter Kenny Dorham, who was then replaced by Donald Byrd.

Because this was initially a group without a single leader, their first album happened to be made under Horace Silver's name

(*Horace Silver And The Jazz Messengers*, Blue Note) and it included two of his most popular compositions, "Doodlin'" and "The Preacher". An inevitable split loomed in 1956, whereby Art retained the Messengers brand name and formed the first of his long series of new groups, while Horace and the three others left to form their own band – with lasting success on all sides. But, in the couple of months before that event, the quintet with Blakey and Silver recorded this classic album, which has all its elements in balance: the attractive original compositions, the effervescent solo work, and the fiery back-seat driving of both pianist and drummer.

Though he takes relatively few solos, Blakey's full panoply of quirky effects can be heard frequently, from the sudden tom-tom punctuations to military drum-rolls which erupt from nowhere, and they always make sense in terms of enhancing whatever's happening at the moment. In addition, several of the original pieces first recorded here capitalize on Art's many different ways of employing Latin rhythms and contrasting them with straight-ahead swing, for instance on Mobley's **Hank's Symphony** and **Carol's Interlude** (included in two versions on this reissue) or Silver's two tunes. The latter two, namely **Ecaroh** and the eleven-minute **Nica's Dream** – dedicated to the Baroness, friend of Blakey, Parker and Thelonious Monk – are among the Messengers' most lasting contributions to the jazz repertoire.

This was the period which first established what became known as "hard-bop" (not coincidentally, the title of Blakey's next album) and led to classic "soul-jazz" hits such as the title track of *Moanin'* and "Dat Dere" from Blakey's *The Big Beat* (Blue Note). The listener-friendly simplification of some of bebop's horn language of 1940s bebop, plus foregrounding its typical rhythmic interaction, are also seen in two pop-song standards treated here, **It's You Or No One** and **The End Of A Love Affair**. The power and wit of the whole approach, along with the melodic lyricism of the young Byrd and Mobley, make this an album very much of its era, but still fresh as a daisy.

⟳We almost chose **Moanin'**, Blue Note, 1999 [1958]

Carla Bley

Escalator Over The Hill

JCOA, 1998 (rec. 1968–71)

Bley (piano, keyboards, organ, calliope, vocals), with various ensembles including Don Cherry (trumpet), Michael Mantler (trumpet, keyboards, synth), Roswell Rudd (trombone), Dewey Redman (alto-sax), Gato Barbieri (tenor-sax), John McLaughlin (guitar), Charlie Haden (bass), Jack Bruce (electric-bass, vocals), Paul Motian (drums), Linda Ronstadt, Jeanne Lee, Paul Jones (vocals), Viva (narration).

Meriting the description "jazz-opera", **Escalator Over The Hill**'s uniqueness extends to being a major composition inspired unequivocally by 1960s hippiedom. Author and free-jazz fan Paul Haines spent much time in India (where else?), posting lyrics to Carla Bley who, as she said, would put them on the piano and "stare at them for hours. I began to feel as if I was reading poetry, with the resulting music as the painstaking by-product of revelation."

Released by coincidence at the same time as *Tommy*, The Who's rock opera, it took any number of recording sessions between 1968 and 1971 to complete. There were overdubs galore, and – although she adapted it much later for public performance, with Haines himself handling the narrative links read here by the actress Viva – a live show was very far from Bley's mind. Then, she was writing for a pool of top talent that included Don Cherry, Roswell Rudd and Gato Barbieri.

The latter two soloists dominate the imposing **Hotel Overture**: this introduces elements from the main work, during which both melodies and musicians will identify different characters in the best Wagnerian tradition. Ignoring unities of time and space, the action switches between a grotty New York hotel, represented by an eerie waltz, and the Indian subcontinent, the gossamer plot revolving around the relationship between Ginger (Linda Ronstadt/Jeanne Lee) and Jack (Bruce). Impenetrable, perhaps, but enhanced massively by the setting – how many operas, after all, derive their enduring appeal from the libretto?

A trombonist who skipped apparently straight from Dixieland to the avant-garde, Rudd's tonal resources are utilized straight away during the mournful opening motif. Barbieri counters at once, his expressive, fruity tenor sax perhaps even more crucial to giving *Escalator* an identity. Comparisons with Stan Getz may seem far-fetched, but both excel at presenting a tune, in Barbieri's case via a broad and gravelly tone that grows incandescent as he stretches for the high notes. Sizzling examples halfway through the "Overture" presage his spot in **Smalltown Agonist**, the final track on the first of the two CDs.

That divide indicates a change of emphasis, the second half more redolent of India. Increasingly committed to what became known as World Music, Cherry stretches out over the clip-clopping rhythms, starting roughly at the point reached by Miles Davis in his Spanish phase. On **Rawalpindi Blues**, a clash between Western jazz-rock and the more contemplative East, his rugged-but-clear tone and occasional scatter-gun phrasing have never gripped harder. As the Westerners, John McLaughlin and Bruce also excel on this piece.

We have since learned to relish Bley's musical combination of what she describes as "possibilities other than happiness" and an acute sense of parody. Apart from the Indian sections and the dance-band routines recreated most faithfully on the **Holiday In Risk Theme** track, she throws in real operatics via soprano Rosalind Hupp who, in common no doubt with others, must have wondered what on earth she was singing. Bley balanced a liking for voices that "cracked, or that wobbled when they held a note" against the need for professionals in certain roles, so she invited Ronstadt and Bruce and welcomed Paul Jones. They do a splendid job, with Ronstadt's **Why** being *Escalator's* one true aria.

⮑ We almost chose **The Very Big Carla Bley Band**, ECM/Watt, 1991 [1990]

Anthony Braxton

For Alto

Delmark, 2000 (rec. 1968)

Braxton (alto-sax).

Revising basic notions about instrumentation in jazz was one of the great challenges musicians tackled in the post-free-jazz period. Without the tacit assumption of a front line backed by rhythm section, a brave new world of formats emerged, including drummerless groups and all-percussion ensembles, saxophone quartets, chamber nonets and gargantuan orchestras.

The concept of playing unaccompanied jazz on reed instruments wasn't new when Anthony Braxton recorded **For Alto** in 1968 – precedents included Coleman Hawkins' celebrated 1948 piece "Picasso" and the early 1960s bass-clarinet versions of "God Bless The Child" by Eric Dolphy. There had even been a full-length solo saxophone album by Bengt "Frippe" Nordström, issued earlier in 1968. But Braxton really put the format on the map. He recorded himself privately, and then issued his findings on Chicago's Delmark Records, as part of a historically crucial series documenting the music of the emerging Association for the Advancement of Creative Musicians (AACM). *For Alto* proved beyond contention what a rich menu one could derive from a lone saxophone.

Long unavailable – Braxton once voiced a fear that it would appear only as a memorial release – the double LP was recently reissued as a single CD. Its sound quality is amateurish, with serious distortion problems, but even heard against a backdrop of brilliant subsequent solo sax records by Evan Parker, Julius Hemphill, Steve Lacy and Joe McPhee, Braxton's remains one of the boldest statements of independence ever waxed. It kicks off with a 37-second lyrical snippet, **Dedicated To Multi-instrumentalist Jack Gell**, followed by a merciless ten-minute dedication to John Cage that's anything but silent. This track should be enough to disprove the frequent characterization of Braxton as excessively brainy – it is corporeal music, forceful and sweaty, straight from the gut, displaying an ecstatic overdrive the ferocity of which rivals Albert Ayler and Peter Brötzmann. A piece for Cecil Taylor contains surprisingly boppish, nearly bluesy phrasing: here you can taste Braxton's special choppy staccato flow, his personal form of groove, evident on the many records where he interprets standards. (Seek out, for prime example, his *Charlie Parker Project 1993*.) **Dedicated To Susan Axelrod** is a post-Dolphy ballad, melodic lines stretched into unforeseen shapes, barely containing themselves, suddenly gushing forth in a cascade of arpeggios.

Braxton is always attendant to structure; his compositions for ensemble (particularly his quartet with Marilyn Crispell, for instance on the album *Willisau (Quartet) 1991*) embed imagination, improvisation and experimentation in a flexible but finite context of organization. On *For Alto*, Braxton explores the extreme parts of the alto, assembling a checklist of materials that he investigates with a scientist's rigour. On **To Artist Murray Pillars**, he uses trills in myriad ways: sweet flutters, oscillation between disjunct notes with rude interjections. **To My Friend Kenny McKenny** combines grumbled low notes, piercing multiphonics and split tones, cataloguing a set of the harshest sax effects. Braxton's interest in clarinettist Jimmy Giuffre is evident on **Dedicated To Ann And Peter Allen**, a study of low-dynamic intensity that involves breath noises and keypad sounds. The final piece, dedicated to violinist Leroy Jenkins, is a twenty-minute landmark, full of unlike elements – halting silences, indelicate honks and squeals, whispered love notes – all abruptly juxtaposed.

Braxton has made self-documentation a priority. He's recorded alone periodically over the last thirty years, continuing to hone these germinal ideas, but *For Alto* remains his great solo masterpiece in the rough.

⮑We almost chose **Willisau (Quartet) 1991**, hat ART, 1992 [1991]

Clifford Brown

Clifford Brown/Max Roach

Verve, 2000 (rec. 1954–55)

Brown (trumpet), Roach (drums), Harold Land (tenor-sax), Richie Powell (piano), George Morrow (bass).

Trumpeter Clifford Brown was first talked about on the musicians' grapevine at the end of the 1940s – just as it seemed that the initial surge of bebop was on the wane. Before he turned twenty, he had earned the admiration and encouragement of Charlie Parker, Dizzy Gillespie, Max Roach, Miles Davis and Fats Navarro. It was the Navarro trumpet style that Brown's most nearly resembled, but what impressed all these expert observers was his ability to play complex ideas, not merely accurately but with a joyous vitality beyond the reach of most other second-generation beboppers.

It took another couple of years, including sixteen months touring with the r&b band of Chris Powell and the Blue Flames, before Brownie moved to New York and the big time. Work with the medium-large band of Tadd Dameron and the very large band of Lionel Hampton led to an initial burst of small-group recordings, including several done in France and Sweden with mixed American–European line-ups while on tour in Europe in 1953. These created the same buzz among listeners as his earliest work had among fellow players, and his subsequent appearance on a famous Art Blakey session (*A Night At Birdland Vols. 1 and 2*) further enhanced his impact.

At this point in the spring of 1954 the young veteran of bebop's first generation, drummer Max Roach, was finishing a six-month contract replacing Shelly Manne at the Los Angeles club the

Lighthouse and, launching his own new group, summoned Brown to be the co-leader. The other sidemen were all LA-based, among them saxist Teddy Edwards and pianist Carl Perkins – soon replaced by Harold Land and temporary resident Richie Powell (younger brother of fellow pianist, Bud) – and their first recording for producer Gene Norman, at present unavailable, awaits a properly mastered unedited reissue. It was immediately clear, however, that Roach and Brownie had a natural empathy and were intent on creating an energetic but unified group sound.

Clifford was easily the most impressive soloist in the band, as is clearly heard on this first studio album. His melodic gift is not only evident in his improvisations (backed up by the addition of three alternate takes), but also in his written lines **Daahoud** and the immortal **Joy Spring** – in this respect, his choice of outside material such as the scale-based **Parisian Thoroughfare** (composed by Powell the elder) and Duke Jordan's **Jor-Du** is also revealing. But Roach's work here established him as the most inventive drummer yet, whose solos also have significant melodic content and whose backings make excellent use of brushes throughout the dynamic "Joy Spring" and mallets on the film theme **Delilah**, as well as sticks elsewhere. Also worth noting are the understated contributions of Land and Powell's almost funky piano on "Delilah" and **The Blues Walk**.

Sadly, Brownie didn't live to see the popularization of the term "hard-bop" – he died, along with Powell and Powell's wife, in a car accident at the age of 25 – but his compositions and the interaction with Roach did much to prepare the ground for it, while their extended intro and coda on "Parisian" prefigures the arrival of "modal jazz". During his brief career, the trumpeter had already fulfilled the promise of the equally short-lived Fats Navarro and, as such, provided an appealing alternative to the then-ascendant Miles Davis. There is no need for such comparisons, however, to highlight Clifford's qualities, whether savouring his recordings with Sarah Vaughan, Helen Merrill and Dinah Washington or this still stunning album.

⮑We almost chose **With Strings,** Verve, 1998 [1955]

Dave Brubeck

Time Out

Columbia, 1997 (rec. 1959)

Brubeck (piano), Paul Desmond (alto-sax), Gene Wright (bass), Joe Morello (drums).

The role of the popularizer is a problem in the context of a book like this. Some of them – Benny Goodman in the swing era, or Stan Getz at the time of the bossa nova – had been perfecting their art for ages, and just happened to be in the right place at the right time. Others, who start out as dedicated impecunious jazzmen, get a taste of popularity and then court it shamelessly, eventually becoming so smooth they no longer generate enough friction to stay upright (for example, Grover Washington, though some would argue he was a stronger musical personality than that).

Dave Brubeck falls into neither of these categories. Emerging from the postwar San Francisco scene, he always followed his own nose and, by dint of hard work, gradually created a new and broader audience for the whole field of "modern jazz". By opening up the college circuit and lending his support to the new 1950s phenomenon of open-air festivals, he indirectly benefited the careers of many fellow musicians. Yet he never impressed his colleagues on the level of sheer ability, and was never notably influential. His early octet had trodden similar ground to Miles Davis's *Birth Of The Cool* band but in a rather lifeless manner, his collective improvisations with altoist Paul Desmond were inferior to those of Gerry Mulligan and others, and the large-scale compositions of his later career have left jazzers and classical musicians unimpressed.

Even his odd-numbered time signatures, which captured the imagination of a wide public, were hardly original. The quartet's waltz-time improvisation on "Some Day My Prince Will Come" (*Dave Digs Disney*, 1957) was preceded by Max Roach and Sonny Rollins's album *Jazz In 3/4 Time* and their earlier version of "Love Is A Many Splendoured Thing", including bars of 5/4. Brubeck's **Time Out** album was in many ways more straightforward than Roach's in presenting its unusual metres (with Dave's relentless repetition of the backing figure in **Take Five** only the most obvious example). Any ability to be polyrhythmic within the metre is heard less frequently, Joe Morello's playing drumming during "Take Five" and Paul Desmond's sax elsewhere being the chief exceptions.

Yet there's an undoubted charm in the overall sound and in the detail of the quartet's performances. The leader's chording, even in improvised solos and in the theme-statement of **Blue Rondo A La Turk**, is more mellow than in his manic early period, and his single-note lines are relaxed and often genuinely inventive. Still, they're no match for Desmond, who, like the best jazz players, seems to be able to get an instant grasp of any situation (rhythmic or chordal) and act as if he'd been in the situation all his life – by this stage, indeed, after a decade's association with Brubeck, it must have *felt* like that, too – and his graceful, witty contributions are ultimately what justify these situations in the first place. The fact that the one tune he contributed was "Take Five" seems to be poetic justice.

Brubeck required his rhythm section, rather as pianist Lennie Tristano did, to lay down a beat and stay out of the way. The fact that the beat was in 9/8 on the opening "Blue Rondo A La Turk" (with a 4/4 middle section) or 6/4 (on **Pick Up Sticks**) or with sections in 3/4 (both **Three To Get Ready** and **Kathy's Waltz**) didn't affect their ability to do just that. And there's something rather comforting for listeners of all persuasions in the fact that the most laidback tracks, **Everybody's Jumpin'** and **Strange Meadowlark** (which later had lyrics added by Brubeck's wife, Iola), lope along in a perfectly normal four-to-the-bar.

⮑We almost chose **Jazz At Oberlin**, OJC, 1987 [1953]

Benny Carter

Further Definitions

Impulse, 1997 (rec. 1961 and 1966)

Benny Carter Phil Woods, Bud Shank (alto-sax), Coleman Hawkins, Charlie Rouse, Buddy Collette, Bill Perkins, Teddy Edwards (tenors), Bill Hood (baritone), Dick Katz, Don Abney (piano), John Collins, Barney Kessel, Mundell Lowe (guitar), Jimmy Garrison, Ray Brown (bass), Jo Jones, Alvin Stoller (drums).

In the year 2001 Benny Carter is still alive, healthy and performing, a fact that would be remarkable enough on its own, even if he didn't happen to be – by common consent – one of the three greatest alto saxophonists in American jazz (the other two were Johnny Hodges and Charlie Parker). Less sensuous and blues-soaked than Hodges, less angular and challenging than his bebop junior, Parker, a Benny Carter solo promises fluent melodic inspiration delivered with urbane grace, degree-level harmonic acknowledgment, sprung rhythm, and a tone that suggests bouquets of bright-white flowers.

It has done so now continuously since the mid-1920s, when Carter's career began with spells in bands led by (amongst others) Charlie Johnson and Horace and Fletcher Henderson. At this time he began arranging, too, took up the trumpet in the early 1930s, and from then on worked consistently both in America and Europe (1935–38) as bandleader and respected master of his craft in others' company. Carter's pre-eminent career, however – devoid of public scandal or self-destructive tendencies – has remained a model of musical dedication and professionalism married to supreme gifts. His achievements as performer, arranger, leader and composer (including prolific composition for films and TV from 1943) are deservingly chronicled in a two-volume work, *Benny Carter*, by Berger, Berger and Patrick (1982), but for the purposes of this small book it's simpler to quote Ira Gitler's assertion that Carter, by the early 1990s, was "the most versatile, continuously active artist in jazz history, and arguably the most honored and talented".

Like everything else about him, Carter's discography is of a consistently high standard, and every listener will have his favourites, but there is perhaps no automatic single choice. One that comes close, nevertheless, is **Further Definitions**, which he recorded in New York in 1961. Already acknowledged as the master arranger for his first instrument, Carter's group for this date consisted simply of four saxophonists – Charlie Rouse, Phil Woods and a lifelong colleague, Coleman Hawkins – along with a similarly well-matched rhythm section, including drummer Jo Jones. The idea had a classic precedent in a 1937 Hawkins recorded date with his European All Star Jam Band (including Django Reinhardt), for which Carter both played and wrote fleet scores on **Honeysuckle Rose** and **Crazy Rhythm**, and these two arrangements are replayed here amid a beautifully recorded and produced session. Carter's luxuriant saxophone-writing is devoured by his A team, in which the dry-toned Rouse and Parker-inflected work of Woods are perfect foils for the senior constituents, who regularly reannounce their supremacy.

Carter's fleet saxophonic grace is at peak form, unsurprisingly pushing Coleman Hawkins to new heights, notably on an exquisite reading of Quincy Jones' **The Midnight Sun Will Never Set**, where the tenorist's solo entry, after eight ensemble bars, is alone worth the price of the record. The two of them are level pegging on "Crazy Rhythm" too, and titles like **Blue Star** (with its double-time last chorus) perfectly illustrate Carter's master skills as arranger. In short, the whole date is a joyful classic. Eight more tracks from 1966 (first issued as *Additions To Further Definitions*) lack the vintage wine of Hawkins, but constitute a super-competent echo of date number one.

➲We almost chose **Benny Carter: The Verve Small Group Sessions**, Verve, 1991 [1954–55]

Betty Carter

Feed The Fire

Verve, 1994 (rec. 1993)

Betty Carter (vocals), Geri Allen (piano), Dave Holland (bass), Jack DeJohnette (drums).

In the late 1940s, Betty Carter worked with Lionel Hampton's band. Over the next thirty years, during which her achievements did not register beyond the very hip, she became a serious cult figure. She sang a chorus on King Pleasure's "Red Top", an early vocalese classic. Some years later, Ray Charles invited her to make an album of duets. Sarah Vaughan gave her the opening half of a concert. Eventually, it all clicked and, almost overnight, everyone began raving about her.

Jazz vocalists have a reputation for doing strange things to a song as written, but nobody takes this to the same extremes. A compulsive improviser, she can distort a tune, hold back words far beyond the point of no return and pick a tempo never dreamt of by the composer. A clue comes from the title of a recent album, *It's Not About The Melody*. By keeping no more than the outline of the original tune, she can twist the lyric so its components forge new relationships, with frequently startling results.

As little-known members of her trio blossomed (former pianists alone include John Hicks, Mulgrew Miller, Benny Green and Stephen Scott), Carter earned a reputation for spotting talent. Recorded live during a tour, **Feed The Fire**, however, was an all-star affair. Sometimes these don't come off, but here expectations were, if anything, exceeded. Each accompanist reaches optimum form, while the discipline imposed by relatively untested routines − not just playing alongside different musicians but duetting with each of them – may have helped Carter concentrate even harder. As usual, the performance gains from an audience egging her on.

To back her exhilarating musicianship, she has a good (though not excessive) range. Compared to many singers, let alone to someone with Sarah Vaughan's vocal presence, the texture of her voice is nothing special – a blessing, perhaps, insofar as it forces her to make an impact by other means. She became, for a start, the nonpareil scat singer, capable of sustaining interest over several choruses. Instead of just piling on syllables she invents diphthongs, uses space, varies dynamics and brings the accompanists in and out of the frame. The technique is realized superbly on the title track, a composition by Geri Allen that lasts over eleven minutes and where everyone solos, and on Carter's improvised duet with Jack DeJohnette called **What Is This Tune?**

Her treatment of **Lover Man** pulls the tempo right down and exaggerates the tune's minor-key feeling. In the process, she drags the lyrics back so far that not all the words fit. The melody of **I'm All Smiles** survives reasonably intact, as she caps the song's essentially theatrical message by a riveting top note at the end. Around Dave Holland's fine solo on their duet on **All Or Nothing At All**, she also stays reasonably close until the lengthy coda, a delicious mix of words and scat. By contrast, she jettisons the tune of **If I Should Lose You**, a gripping, virtually out-of-tempo duet with Allen. After staying relatively faithful to **Day Dream** at the start, again taken very slowly, she skirts round the modulations of a bridge that most singers would cling to. An oddly accented passage built into the opening eight bars of **Sometimes I'm Happy** gets pulled all over the place and, after a typically abrasive solo from Allen, becomes the springboard for a jubilant finale

Snippets of scat on a closing blues to clear the stage are common enough, but few leave the audience in better spirits than those sung here by Betty Carter.

⮑We almost chose **The Audience With Betty Carter**, Verve, 1989 [1979]

Charlie Christian

1939–41: Genius Of Electric Guitar

Giants Of Jazz, 1998 (rec. 1939–41)

Christian (electric guitar), with groups including Cootie Williams, Buck Clayton (trumpet), Benny Goodman, Edmond Hall (clarinet), Georgie Auld, Lester Young (tenor-sax), Lionel Hampton (vibraphone), Count Basie, Johnny Guarnieri (piano), Meade 'Lux' Lewis (celeste) et al.

Charlie Christian (b. July 29, 1916) shares with his contemporary Jimmy Blanton one of the shortest, yet most innovative, careers in jazz. Blanton set new and brilliant standards for the double bass as it would develop throughout the 1940s and 1950s modern jazz generation, and Christian, who died (like Blanton) in 1942 at only 25, did the same for electric guitar.

Before him, the instrument had been pioneered by Eddie Durham, but it was Christian's genius that brought it into public focus. His mathematically accurate rhythmic lines, melodic and harmonic perfection and fat, satisfying amplified tone were the inspiration for a generation of younger guitarists, including Barney Kessel, Jim Hall, Jimmy Raney and Kenny Burrell. And it was only the full-scale emergence of the guitar-based rock generation in the 1960s (and the transformation of the instrument itself) which would create a new school of players like John Scofield or Pat Metheny and set Christian's central contribution to jazz history in conclusive perspective.

Benny Goodman first hired Christian following a legendary jam session at the Victor Hugo Hotel in Beverly Hills in the summer of 1939, and a year or so later pianist Mel Powell brought the young guitarist to Minton's Playhouse – the club on 118th Street, New York, where the roots of bebop were developing at Monday night jam sessions. Christian played there regularly, and informal live recordings from 1941 (with, amongst others, Thelonious Monk, Kenny Clarke and trumpeter Joe Guy) reveal that, given time, he would probably have emerged as a central figure in the bebop revolutions of Monk, Parker and Gillespie that blossomed by 1945. As it is, Christian's rich recorded legacy is principally to be found with Goodman, in the company of the premier stars of the swing era, and most of his best sides are contained in this excellent budget-label **Genius Of Electric Guitar** compilation.

With Goodman's full orchestra, he made two remarkable sides – **Honeysuckle Rose** (in November 1939) and the definitive **Solo Flight** from March 1941 (both here) – but equally essential are the small-group sides, beginning in October 1939 with a relaxed **Flying Home** and **Stardust**, on which Christian's classic last chorus – measured, chordally ingenious and with a wicked quote from "Pretty Baby" thrown in – is the record's deserving climax. In addition, the collection has nineteen more tracks, amongst them seven classics by Goodman's sextet, including trumpeter Cootie Williams (growling disconsolately above the vivacious **Wholly Cats** and equally spritely **Breakfast Feud**, and making a further definitive contribution to **As Long As I Live**) and the great tenorist Georgie Auld. Christian is all over these sides, soloing with consistent brilliance and providing substantial rhythm guitar which fattens his section up without slowing it down. The regular presence of Count Basie adds economic jewellery to the rhythm section, too, on the well-remembered **Till Tom Special**, for example, and **Gone With "What" Wind** (from February 1940 with Lionel Hampton); on "Till Tom Special", Christian's solo returning on a minor sixth, after Basie's middle eight, is a fine illustration of his "swing-to-bop" approach. Other equally essential classics here include **Airmail Special** and **A Smooth One**, plus two fine 1940 titles with Lester Young and Buck Clayton (**I Never Knew** and **Lester's Dream**) and the attractive **Profoundly Blue** by Edmond Hall's quartet (with Meade "Lux" Lewis on celeste), making this the best and most generous CD illustration of Christian's work you can buy.

⮑We almost chose **After Hours**, OJC, 2000 [1941]

Ornette Coleman

Change Of The Century

Atlantic, 1992 (rec. 1959)

Coleman (alto-sax), Don Cherry (pocket-trumpet), Charlie Haden (bass), Billy Higgins (drums).

Ornette Coleman recorded a paradigm-shifting series of six quartet records for Atlantic between 1959 and 1962, each a classic in its own right. The group's line-ups changed slightly over the course of these sessions, but the first of the quartets – with bassist Charlie Haden, drummer Billy Higgins and Coleman's crucial partner Don Cherry on the foreshortened pocket trumpet – set the trend with two utterly fresh LPs. Their Atlantic debut, *The Shape Of Jazz To Come*, contains "Lonely Woman", Ornette's contribution to the jazz standard repertoire, but it's the group's second outing that takes the cake.

Change Of The Century was recorded in Hollywood in October 1959, just a few weeks before the group played their controversial first dates in New York. Forty-plus years later, it is difficult to hear what all the hubbub was about at the time, but the coming of Ornette was discussed among some hard-bop hardliners as a scourge against reason and a threat to civilization. The source of this trepidation was Coleman's liberated concept of melody and its relation to harmony. Some commentators have mistakenly suggested that Coleman dispensed with harmony altogether when he jettisoned the primary chordal instrument, the piano. In truth, most of his pieces are still harmonically based (one could, if pressed, put chords under the heads), a point made immediately evident by following the bass on a piece like the jubilant **Bird Food**. Haden may not spell the cycle of changes as religiously as Ray Brown, but he's definitely locked in on a basic tonal territory. Coleman and Cherry, too, orbit around key-centres, grafting melodic lines together in ways that attend as much to the expressive potential of a phrase as to the theoretical legality of that line in the courtroom of functional harmony.

Coleman's quartets were profoundly creative ensembles, expanding the bounds of swing-based, conventionally formatted jazz. The proper term for their music is "freebop", rather than free jazz, as Higgins' drumming maintains a propulsive, metrical time feel, pieces are structured with written heads and strings of solos, and the tunes have a quick, linear, boppish sensibility. Coleman's compositions brim with joy – check the funky bass-line and calypso undercurrent of **Una Muy Bonita**, and the folksy downhome blues of **Ramblin'**, replete with Haden's famous quotation of "Turkey In The Straw". Coleman and Cherry were one of the great tag-teams in jazz, ricocheting ideas off the bubbling rhythm section, picking up on one another's thoughts and finishing each other's sentences. Listen to them exchange economical lines on Haden's feature, **The Face Of The Bass**. Cherry's solo is ingenious in its clarity and simplicity, from a singsong, childlike opening to the baton pass, after which Coleman is boundlessly playful, gobbling up the wicked swing like a kid in a sonic sweet shop.

Free starts with the horns hopping on a magnificent roller-coaster up and down a couple of scales, into solos over scalding time. Haden stops to play only intermittent, slow-motion notes, then bursts back into the uptempo Higgins undertow, laying out again, letting the horns work with the drums; it's an effect not unlike a good mix in dub reggae, foiling expectations spontaneously. Coleman's keening white plastic alto is tremendous throughout. Listen to the way he varies the dynamic on **Forerunner** – like he's having a conversation with himself, between the brash and the soft-spoken sides of his personality.

⊃We almost chose **The Shape Of Jazz To Come**, Atlantic, 1987 [1959]

John Coltrane

Giant Steps

Atlantic, 1987 (rec. 1959)

Coltrane (tenor-sax), Tommy Flanagan, Cedar Walton, Wynton Kelly (piano), Paul Chambers (bass), Art Taylor, Lex Humphries, Jimmy Cobb (drums).

The recording career of saxophonist John Coltrane is often delineated in terms of his record label affiliations. Aside from his work with Miles Davis and his famous Blue Note record, *Blue Trane*, the bulk of early Coltrane can be divided between his output for Prestige – a varied, often brilliant oeuvre during which his accretive, permutational, glissando-like solos earned the label "sheets of sound" – and his crucial sessions for Atlantic, with whom he signed in 1959.

The recordings Coltrane made for the company – which had moved fairly recently into jazz after a decade of success in blues and r&b – over a two-year period resulted in eight separate LPs. Some of these, like his fascinating take on Ornette Coleman's compositions with trumpeter Don Cherry, *The Avant Garde*, were only issued years after they were waxed. If you've got a fair bit of extra change, the seven-CD collection of the complete Atlantic Coltrane, *The Heavyweight Champion*, is well worth the investment.

Giant Steps is the culmination of early Trane, and it's one of the milestones of modern jazz. For many young jazz musicians, the title track remains a sort of totem of technical achievement, a ring to reach for, a litmus test for aspiring hard-core jazz saxophonists and piano players. Taken at a harrowing clip, it's built on a kaleidoscopic chord sequence. On the originally issued take,

Coltrane gobbles up the tricky changes with relish, bounding forward impetuously – indeed, this was the first record on which he featured only his own compositions, which he was crafting to his advanced musical concept's precise specifications. On the reissued CD, an alternate take of **Giant Steps** (included along with second versions of four other tracks as well) features the otherwise excellent pianist Cedar Walton struggling to make it through the exacting tune. Even on the released version, the great Tommy Flanagan gets a bit hung up in his solo. If jazz has something in common with sport, this piece is perhaps its most dangerous game.

For those thrilled by the sheer vertigo of "Giant Steps", there's also the quicksilver **Countdown**, a similarly structured sprint that saves the theme for the very end. The first minute features a drum and tenor duet so breathless that it seems to dare the rest of the band to join in. The date contains several more of Coltrane's best-known pieces. **Syeeda's Song Flute** features a nifty little syncopation in the head that gives the saxophonist plenty to chew on in his keening solo. On the slow, rapturous ballad **Naima**, Coltrane's glorious tone is in plain view – luminous, very sparing on vibrato, tight, hard-edged, but still sweet. The stunning coda of seven long notes is worth the price of admission alone.

Mr. P.C. was written for Paul Chambers, one of the finest bassists of all time, and it spotlights Chambers's impeccable beat, light touch, big sound and total command of the changes. He and drummer Art Taylor propel the session self-effacingly, but with absolute authority. Like **Cousin Mary** – another perfect vehicle for Coltrane's unfurling superposed melodic lines – "Mr. P.C." is a blues, offering a link to the more conventional hard-bop of Coltrane's Prestige days. Yet in the saxophonist's solos on these tracks his speed, clarity, and especially his harmonic ingenuity, point the way to the next phase of his career, in which he would take these dazzling artistic feats to another plane altogether.

⮑ We almost chose **Plays The Blues**, Atlantic, 1989 [1960]

21

John Coltrane

A Love Supreme

Impulse!, 1995 (rec. 1964)

Coltrane (tenor-sax), McCoy Tyner (piano), Jimmy Garrison (bass), Elvin Jones (drums).

The John Coltrane Quartet is, along with the Charles Mingus Quintet and the Miles Davis Quintet, one of the most profound working groups in the history of jazz after bebop. The Coltrane foursome assembled piecemeal between 1960 and 1961, when Garrison joined; they subsequently toured and recorded together non-stop until 1965, sometimes with the addition of another horn player, such as Eric Dolphy or Archie Shepp. Together, on classic records made for the Impulse! label, the group documented the saxophonist-leader's avowed religious quest and his increasingly radiant horn-work. But the most important thing they did was as a unit; theirs was a true group music, something emanating from the experience of playing together night after night over a long period, sharing discoveries and venturing together into totally uncharted waters.

By the time the group formed, Coltrane had taken his craft on the tenor (and later soprano) saxophone to unheard-of realms, setting out and overcoming massive technical and theoretical challenges, continually pushing himself into fresh turf. After the hyper-complexity of *Giant Steps*, Coltrane began to grow reductive. Influenced by the world's great modal improvising traditions, like Indian classical and Arabic musics, he expanded on Miles's modal jazz, deeply exploring the possibilities of restricted harmonic motion. But Coltrane's music was always very sophisticated in terms of harmony, and even his most static, simple, reduced modal investigations, like those on **A Love Supreme**, contain a wellspring of harmonic implications.

Recorded in 1964, towards the end of the quartet's lifespan, *A Love Supreme* is a four-part spiritual suite. The first section, **Acknowledgement**, sets out the now-famous four-note motif; while Coltrane runs the figure through various keys, Jimmy Garrison's bass hugs closely to the tone centre – an open exposition on modality. At the section's close, the group sings the title words in the notes of the main melody. The combination of text/melodic theme will recur later, in a different form. In part two, **Resolution**, McCoy Tyner demonstrates the personal style that left its mark on several generations of piano players – big, thunderous, widely voiced chords in the left hand and a scampering linear right hand, aggressively pushing harmonic substitutions nearly to the point of tonal collapse. This is the quartet in top form, archetypical, Trane's tenor soaring majestically, Elvin Jones deftly keeping time on cymbal and meanwhile creating mounting tension with triplets on the snare.

The third and fourth sections, **Pursuance** and **Psalm** respectively, run together as a continuous track on the record. "Pursuance" starts with a drum solo, then leaps into a buoyant, uptempo gallop. At this time, in concert Coltrane's solos were often epic, raga-like in length, so the tenor spot here is, by comparison, a compact three minutes, but it's a jam-packed one, brimming with rhythmic and melodic excitement. Garrison's unaccompanied solo acts as a bridge to the finale; he was a master of chording the bass, with a trademark flamenco strum to which he turns in the middle of the supple solo. Elvin plays "Psalm" with mallets, rolling like timpani. In the notes, Coltrane calls the piece "a musical narration of the theme 'A Love Supreme'", a poem that's included in the booklet. If you listen to the melody and follow the words of the poem, it turns out that he's articulating the syllables of the text, like a wordless cantor intoning the spiritual message. An intense combination of serenity and epiphany, this through-composed section is unique in the jazz repertoire.

⮩We almost chose **Ballads**, Impulse!, 1995 [1962]

22

Eddie Condon

The Chronological Eddie Condon 1944–46

Classics, 1998 (rec. 1944–46)

Condon (rhythm guitar), with groups including Billy Butterfield, Bobby Hackett, Wild Bill Davison, Max Kaminsky (trumpet), Jack Teagarden, Lou McGarity (trombone), Brad Gowans (valve-trombone), Pee Wee Russell, Bud Freeman, Ernie Caceres (reeds), James P Johnson, Jess Stacy (piano).

Guitarist Eddie Condon was the figurehead (as well the lifelong spokesman) for the school of jazz known as "Chicago-style". Originally a white echo of black originators (including King Oliver and Armstrong) his music very early on acquired originalities of its own. In due course, he was surrounded by a school of highly skilled cornermen, among them Max Kaminsky, Bobby Hackett, Pee Wee Russell, Bud Freeman, Brad Gowans and Gene Schroeder. Condon himself – a fast-talking witty ambassador for the music, who co-authored three irresistible books about his life, music and colleagues – was a frequently underrated musician (he used a four-stringed instrument tuned like a banjo), but cornettist Bobby Hackett may well have been right in his assertion that "Eddie was the greatest rhythm guitarist you ever heard!"

From 1938, after ten years of freelance recording, Condon signed to Milt Gabler's Commodore label for six years and these classic sides – plus weekly broadcasts for a year for the Blue Network from New York's Town Hall and Ritz Theatre – encouraged him to open his own club in 1945. In 1948 he published his autobiography *We Called It Music* and in 1949 he hosted the *Eddie Condon Floorshow* on television. From then on he was a jazz celebrity for life, whose later records are similarly classics of jazz discography, featuring premier names, many of them celebrated below.

By December 1944 Condon had re-contracted to Decca, a signing which was to produce some of the most ravishing recordings of his career. The occasional rough edges of early Commodore sides had all but gone, and a sense of occasion prevailed that contrasted with the determined (albeit wholly successful) informality of Condon's LP recording of the 1950s. **The Chronological Eddie Condon 1944–46** begins with three V-Disc sides (including Hot Lips Page's earthy **Uncle Sam's Blues**) but by track four the masterpieces have cracked in with **When Your Lover Has Gone**, where the solos, over jazzmaster Hackett's arrangement, are shared between Condon, Jack Teagarden and the great Billy Butterfield. The exquisite **Wherever There's Love** (written by Condon with lyricist John deVries, and sung by Lee Wiley) is next, and from here the joys multiply. High points include: Wiley's dicty sensuality on two Gershwin ballads; Hackett's totally approriate settings and wandering, wondersome cornet framing her vocals with master's taste and inspiration; the ever-gentle Jack Teagarden, whose kingly trombone graces eleven tracks here, and whose lovable and comforting voice graces **Impromptu Ensemble No. 1**, a stylishly routined **Shiek Of Araby**, and **Somebody Loves Me**. (This last, remarkable track is an early masterpiece for Hackett and Teagarden both of whom feature on Hackett's *Coast Concert* (1955) and Teagarden's *Jazz Ultimate* (1957), two wonderful albums that EMI have recently combined on a CD that's every bit as essential as this one.) Hackett's "Somebody Loves Me" solo here is so good it was later re-scored for full-band ensemble by the gifted Dan Barrett (in 1987) and he plays equally beautifully on the lyric solo ballad feature, **My One And Only**. Condon's industrious guitar is regularly audible (notably on **Oh! Lady Be Good**) and by track nineteen (**Farewell Blues**) cornettist Wild Bill Davison has made his welcome roughhouse debut too. Six more indispensable tracks follow in a one-volume masterpiece, which should be thoroughly studied by anyone who still believes that traditional jazz has nothing to do with high art.

⮍We almost chose **Eddie Condon Dixieland All-Stars**,

MCA/GRP, 1994 [1939–46]

23

Chick Corea

Return To Forever

ECM, undated (rec. 1972)

Corea (electric piano), Joe Farrell (flute, soprano-sax), Stanley Clarke (bass, electric bass), Airto Moreira (drums, percussion), Flora Purim (vocals, percussion).

chick corea · return to forever

The fallout from the 1960s was considerable, with the establishment of free-jazz and the explosion of rock music. For at least some younger jazzmen, both of these had considerable appeal, and there were moves to incorporate aspects of rock before Miles Davis gave it his approval. But the philosophical fallout of "peace, love and spirituality" is often overlooked in a jazz context.

The careers of three key musicians bear this out. At the start of the 1970s, Chick Corea was leading the avant-garde quartet Circle containing Anthony Braxton, while Herbie Hancock (with his Sextet) and Wayne Shorter (in the early days of Weather Report) were attempting to combine the rhythms and electrification of rock with unrestricted improvisation. However, after Corea got into Scientology and both Hancock and Shorter espoused a Westernized version of Buddhism, they realized that they were failing to reach a wide enough audience. While Shorter was content to let Weather Report evolve into something new (under the guidance of Joe Zawinul), Corea and Hancock simply disbanded their groups and set off in a new direction.

The band that recorded the album **Return To Forever** turned out to be something of a halfway stage for Corea since, despite turning his back on the Circle era, he had yet to adopt rock-stadium volume levels and the guitar histrionics of such as

Bill Connors and Al DiMeola. The stance of this group was rooted in a combination of electric jazz with Afro-Brazilian music, influenced not only by the inclusion of Airto and his wife Flora Purim but by Corea's previous involvement with Latin bandleaders such as Mongo Santamaria and Herbie Mann. While this outfit was still trying to find its feet, some members were simultaneously involved with Stan Getz, who employed Corea, Clarke and Airto (on auxiliary percussion), plus Tony Williams on drums, and recorded Corea's tune "La Fiesta" on his album *Captain Marvel* (Koch, 1998 [1972]).

The aura of much of the music is created by the combination of the pianist's successful use of a single keyboard (no pedals, no synthesizers) and his distinctive sound – which has much to do with a careful distillation of McCoy Tyner's voicings in order to avoid the muddiness inherent in such chords when played on electric instruments. The material is also coloured by occasional use of Purim's voice, either singing in wordless unison with keyboard on the title suite, or doing her best with the rather sappy lyrics of **What Game Shall We Play Today** and **Sometime Ago**. Airto, in the then-unaccustomed role of kit-drummer, is just unconventional enough to be quite interesting, and Clarke, who stayed with various editions of Corea's band for half a decade, provides considerable energy without distracting from the collective purpose.

The best is saved for last. Farrell, previously heard only on flute and piccolo, plays soprano on the leader's evergreen **La Fiesta**, based on the same scale that everyone uses to suggest a flamenco influence. His playing has a strong Coltrane influence, but whatever toughness there may have been is conveniently ironed out by ECM's recording. Despite the fact that the tune is a medium-fast jazz-waltz, a genre Trane made his own with **My Favourite Things** and others – and that Corea's second theme takes off from Trane's solo on the Miles Davis **Some Day My Prince Will Come** – this is not 1960s angst but 1970s positivity. The optimism is still captivating all these years later.

⮑We almost chose **Now He Sings, Now He Sobs**, Blue Note, 1988 [1968]

24

Bob Crosby

Bob Crosby And His Orchestra: South Rampart Street Parade

MCA/GRP, 1992 (rec. 1936–42)

Featuring Crosby's Orchestra and "Bobcats", including Yank Lawson, Billy Butterfield (trumpet), Ward Silloway, Ray Conniff (trombone), Gil Rodin, Matty Matlock, Irving Fazola, Eddie Miller, Bill Stegmeyer (reeds), Bob Zurke, Joe Sullivan (piano), Nappy Lamare (guitar), Bob Haggart (bass), Ray Bauduc (drums).

Richard Sudhalter's sleeve notes alone are usually worth the price of any CD, and this compilation is no exception. In the course of an informative and thoroughly researched essay, he summarizes the qualities of Bob Crosby's music which separated it from most other bands of the Swing era. As double-bassist Bob Haggart – a cornerman of the orchestra – affirmed to Sudhalter: "Most of the time we didn't pay much attention to what everybody else was doing." And that was because this group of musicians, fronted by the talented brother of Bing Crosby, took their inspiration from Dixieland and fashioned their music accordingly.

Crosby's organization, which operated between 1935 and 1944, centred on a team of premier-league and like-minded players, amongst them trumpeters Yank Lawson and Billy Butterfield, clarinettists Matty Matlock and Irving Fazola, tenorist Eddie Miller, pianist Bob Zurke, guitarist Nappy Lamare, bassist Haggart and drummer Ray Bauduc. Matlock, Haggart and saxophonist Dean Kincaide were the principal arrangers who steered the orchestra's musical output away from standard swing fare. And from November 1937, its band-within-a-band – the eight-piece "Bobcats" – became a principal focus of Crosby's activities by bringing the art of small-group Dixieland to vivacious new heights.

The Bobcats would continue to play long after their parent orchestra ceased to exist, regularly resurfacing for reunions under Crosby's leadership, as well as in similarly definitive fashion (from 1951) as the Lawson-Haggart Jazz Band and, from the 1970s, the aptly (if controversially) dubbed "World's Greatest Jazz Band".

Crosby's orchestra and small group – while universally acknowledged for quality – are not always fully acknowledged as a valid forerunner to the New Orleans jazz Revival of the 1940s. This has partly to do with the level of their collective musical ability which was formidable, and therefore set them apart from the conscious "back to the roots" primitivism which typified both originals, like Bunk Johnson or George Lewis, and late impressionists from Lu Watters on. Nevertheless, several of Crosby's alumni (including Miller, Lamare and Bauduc) were all from New Orleans and the orchestra's output constantly drew on the inspirations of traditional jazz and its repertoire, as well as fashioning brilliant new creations of its own. These include the classic **South Rampart Street Parade**, a dashing contemporary tone poem by Crosby, Haggart and Bauduc, inspired by a New Orleans marching band. But from track one the references are clearly stated: **Dixieland Shuffle** is really a paraphrase of one theme from King Oliver's 1923 "Riverside Blues", and track two – **Royal Garden Blues** – deliberately refers to Bix Beiderbecke's recording of the tune ten years previously. Musical high points include Miller's ever-friendly tenor, carefree clarinet trios mid-score, and Lawson's hectoring trumpet. Butterfield's ravishing feature **What's New** (by Haggart and Johnny Burke) joins others here, including Zurke's headlong **Little Rock Getaway** and Fazola's lyric liquid outing on **My Inspiration**. The bassist's **I'm Prayin' Humble** and later **Chain Gang** vividly illustrate his front-rank arranger's visions, and **Big Noise From Winnetka**, featuring his double bass and whistling along with Bauduc's tom-toms, was to become one of traditional jazz's most revisited features from an orchestra which, in commentator Dave Dexter's words, remains "a truly distinctive and 100 percent original organisation".

➲No Alternative - **nothing else is as comprehensive**

25

Miles Davis

Porgy And Bess

Columbia, 1997 (rec. 1958)

Davis (trumpet, flugelhorn), big band including Bill Barber (tuba), Paul Chambers (bass), Philly Joe Jones, Jimmy Cobb (drums), Gil Evans (arranger, conductor).

The trumpeter whose first exposure was as a timid sideman in Charlie Parker's quintet made up in determination what he lacked in physical stature. Having decided that emulating Dizzy Gillespie's pyrotechnics was not appropriate for his personality (or his technical abilities), he forged a much simpler and more direct style which, as early as the late 1940s, had begun to approach its initial maturity. As a result, he exerted a huge effect on other trumpeters and, for nearly thirty years, the groups he led became even more influential on the way bands played together.

A long series of albums on the Prestige label documents the small groups he fronted, culminating in the sextet he was leading in 1958–59 which created the epoch-making *Kind Of Blue* (Columbia). During the same time frame, however, he was also continuing to explore aspects of his slightly larger group from the late 1940s, hallowed in jazz history as the *"Birth Of The Cool* band" after the album title of its reissued records (Capitol). That band's influence had been somewhat diluted by numerous early 1950s imitations, but Miles (also aware of Duke Ellington's innovations) saw in it new possibilities of featuring his playing against a more orchestral backdrop to be organized by the senior figure among the *BOTC* collaborators, arranger Gil Evans.

An early move in this direction, involving music written by John Lewis and J.J. Johnson, is now incorporated in the reissue, *Birth Of The Third Stream* – "third stream" referring to the frequent attempts to mix equal parts of jazz and classical music and come up with a new compound. Miles's first album with Evans, however, the excellent *Miles Ahead* (both this and *BOTTS* are on Columbia), focused Davis's flugelhorn in a concerto-like setting, with an eclectic repertoire of old pop songs and originals by such as Dave Brubeck, Ahmad Jamal and French composer Léo Delibes. The follow-up took a single source, Gershwin's "early-third-stream" opera, and miraculously turned it into an even more varied emotional experience.

Once again the only horn soloist, Miles now alternated muted trumpet with his flugel and drew more directly on the different approaches developed in his recent small-group work. As well as heartfelt ballads such as **Bess, You Is My Woman Now** and **I Loves You Porgy**, there are medium-tempo grooves on **It Ain't Necessarily So** and **Summertime**. Further distinguishing **Porgy And Bess** from *Miles Ahead* are two uptempo interpretations in **There's A Boat That's Leaving Soon** and **Gone** (on which drummer Philly Joe Jones is featured, and whose slow Gershwin version, **Gone, Gone, Gone**, is also included). Throughout, Evans as arranger responds to his expectations of Davis with wonderful writing, from the variously enunciated riff of "Summertime" to the sensuality of **Oh Bess** to the boppish tuba variation of **The Buzzard Song**.

Though none of them improvise, Evans paid justified tribute to the large brass section, stuffed with studio-experienced but jazz-rooted musicians who could take these adaptations – some of them quite close to Gershwin, on paper – and breathe life into them. Many of the same players were on hand when, the following year, Miles and Gil began the most rarefied of their joint efforts, *Sketches Of Spain* (with its barrier-breaking version of the "Concierto De Aranjuez" and the extraordinary evocation of a Spanish religious ceremony in "Saeta"). Not long after, though they occasionally collaborated again, the interests of the two principals started to diverge, but *Porgy And Bess* and its two companion albums will forever remain timeless achievements.

⊃We almost chose **Sketches Of Spain**, Columbia, 1997 [1959–60]

26

Miles Davis

Kind Of Blue

Columbia, 1997 (rec. 1959)

Davis (trumpet), Cannonball Adderley (alto-sax), John Coltrane (tenor-sax), Bill Evans, Wynton Kelly (piano), Paul Chambers (bass), Jimmy Cobb (drums).

To see someone eagerly clutching an unopened copy of **Kind Of Blue** in the New York subway is a reminder that it continues to haunt the current bestseller lists over forty years after its recording. Improbable though it might seem that there are people who have yet to hear the album, clearly not all the purchases are replacement copies and chances are that many readers of the book would like to be reminded why it's considered so essential.

As implied when discussing his *Porgy And Bess*, most of Miles's self-development took place within the context of his small groups. That of 1955–56 (the quintet featuring John Coltrane and *the* rhythm section – Red Garland, Paul Chambers and Philly Joe Jones) was not the first benchmark he'd established, but it achieved his biggest impact so far by loosening the bonds of the prevailing bop and hard-bop. After a brief diversion during which Miles employed other saxophonists, he had by Christmas 1957 reconvened the famous quintet and added a recent colleague, Cannonball Adderley – Adderley's notable *Somethin' Else* (Blue Note), featuring Davis, is from early 1958, and so is Miles's great sextet album *Milestones* (Columbia). Particularly the non-functional harmony of the Adderley album's title-track blues (plus its counterpart on *Milestones*, "Sid's Ahead") – and, even more so, the Ahmad Jamal-inspired absence of a chord sequence in the track variously issued as "Milestones" or "Miles" – triumphantly confirmed a definitive move away from current practice.

Davis was again ahead of the crowd, putting to work the theories of composer George Russell and improvising on scales rather than chords (hence the term "modal jazz"). But, for all the success of the two previously mentioned 1958 albums, *Kind Of Blue* would not have been possible if Miles hadn't taken on board the subtly swinging Jimmy Cobb (so different from Philly Joe's energy and dynamism) and replaced Garland with the supremely sensitive Bill Evans. That Evans would have an enormous effect on Davis's music was evident from the popular standards they recorded (since reissued as *'58 Sessions*, Columbia). But the *Kind Of Blue* material – which Bill helped to prepare, in the case of **Blue In Green** and **Flamenco Sketches**, while *Gil* Evans wrote the introduction to **So What** – deliberately kicked away the chordal crutches and forced the soloists to concentrate on melodic content.

Setting up a situation in which the structures were minimal, Davis also kept the other sidemen in the dark until they were recording (even conventional material was more often worked on before going into the studio in those days). Forcing a maximum of concentration was the fact that, apart from brief rundowns of the few ensemble passages, only one take was done for four of the pieces, plus two versions of the most open form of all, "Flamenco Sketches" – the current reissue includes all six complete performances. Balancing the contrast between the catchy but minimal hooks and the lack of footholds for improvisation, Davis also ensured that he and Evans were the calm centre of events, while Chambers and Cobb played with more restraint than ever before or since, but Adderley and Coltrane were encouraged to be expansive and even verbose. And, just so the emotional ambience didn't become too distilled, the blues **Freddie Freeloader** used the funky Wynton Kelly, Miles's new pianist, in place of Evans.

The above may describe some of the reasons why *Kind Of Blue* sounds as it does, but ultimately it's impossible to explain one of the unique masterpieces of jazz.

◗We almost chose **Milestones**, Columbia, 2000 [1958]

27

Miles Davis

Bitches Brew

Columbia, 1999 (rec. 1969)

Davis (trumpet), Wayne Shorter (soprano-sax), Bennie Maupin (bass-clarinet), Chick Corea, Larry Young, Joe Zawinul (electric-piano), John McLaughlin (guitar), Dave Holland (bass), Harvey Brooks (electric-bass), Jack DeJohnette, Lonny White (drums), Don Alias, Jumma Santos (Jim Riley) (percussion).

There is an understandable tendency for writers to discuss different periods of Miles Davis through the various musicians working in his bands. This is perhaps a useful antidote to the more naive fan-club approach that ascribes every note on his albums to the genius of Miles alone. Though it's true that his choice of sidemen was often bold to the point of recklessness (from Coltrane onwards), his eye for their potential could only be vindicated by the generous space he then offered them. As some of these players have pointed out, Davis was such an ideal bandleader because (like the early Ellington and few others) he left himself open and vulnerable enough to be able to draw strength from his colleagues.

Just as *Porgy And Bess* and *Kind Of Blue* were a direct outgrowth of Davis's work in, respectively, the late 1940s and the mid-1950s, his equally dramatic "change of style" in 1969 was more like a gradual evolution from 1965 onwards. The quintet he led then, and for the next four years, included Wayne Shorter, Herbie Hancock, Ron Carter and Tony Williams, all pace-setters on their instruments and, in the case of Hancock and Williams, considerably younger than their predecessors. Their excitingly abstract "acoustic" playing was occasionally tempered by a feel for pop music (see *ESP* and *Miles Smiles*), but this was brought front-and-centre by the use of electric piano and bass on such 1968 sessions as *Miles In The Sky* and *Filles De Kilimanjaro* (Hancock and Carter being replaced by Chick Corea and British bassist Dave Holland during the latter).

A concept of "jazz-rock" was being adopted by several rock bands and, from the jazz direction, the Gary Burton and Charles Lloyd groups, which inspired Davis to put his personal stamp on the idea. For recording purposes only, he added two more Europeans, Joe Zawinul and John McLaughlin, on keyboards and guitar – the rock instrument *par excellence* – firstly on *In A Silent Way* and then (hiring Lloyd's young drummer Jack DeJohnette to replace Williams) on the double-CD **Bitches Brew**. *Silent* was relatively cautious, yet sufficiently controversial to guarantee extra marketing for the follow-up, and it was the latter that really broke through to a wider audience. Soon Miles was parading his charisma in rock auditoriums and setting everyone back on their heels, not only purist jazzers but pop fans who had never heard any jazz and wondered what this aggressive music was all about.

The real wonder, in retrospect, is how little compromise Davis made in essence. The thematic material of the title track or Zawinul's **Pharaoh's Dance** is far removed from conventional melodic hooks, the leader's own trumpet is a constantly challenging voice and the use made of guitar and keyboards often reveals the players' backgrounds in free jazz. Davis links back to his earlier work in the bluesy **Miles Runs The Voodoo Down**, which, like several tracks, has an unsettling undercurrent of bass clarinet, and in the ballad **Sanctuary** – which drops the expanded group in favour of his basic quintet. Davis often plays within the rhythm-section rather than on top (so do the other soloists), but that was not a new departure for him.

Further work in this vein showed how rich were the possibilities, for instance on the album *Live-Evil* (credited to "Selim Sivad"!) or the more rhythm-and-blues- and soul-based *Jack Johnson*. But, as well as creating a dynasty of future bandleaders, Davis here set down a benchmark unequalled by any subsequent "fusion music".

⤷We almost chose **Jack Johnson**, Columbia, 1992 [1970]

28

Wild Bill Davison

Pretty Wild/With Strings Attached

Arbors, 2000 (rec. 1956–57)

Davison (trumpet-cornet), with strings, plus (on *With Strings Attached*) Bob Wilber (clarinet), Cutty Cutshall (trombone), Gene Schroeder (piano), Barry Galbraith (guitar), Jack Lesberg (bass), Don Lamond (drums).

Wild Bill Davison, the ebullient cornettist from Defiance, Ohio, is one of jazz's greatest brass voices and best-loved figureheads. "The Wild One", as he was affectionately known, brought his cornet to New York in 1941 to lead his own band at Nick's Club, Greenwich Village, and made classic records for Milt Gabler's Commodore label from 1943 before becoming house cornettist at Eddie Condon's club in 1945. From then on, his playing – a magical meld of roughhouse creativity at uptempo, and soft-toned Irish sentiment on ballads – became an irresistible object of respect and affection to fans and friends. A classic word-portrait of Davison, by Carlton Brown, may be found in *Eddie Condon's Treasury of Jazz* (1957). His powerful passionate style also presented strong and viable alternatives to the artistic parameters set down by Louis Armstrong (although it took some time for the jazz world to catch up with the fact), and in more recent years Davison has been definitively recognized as one of jazz music's most individual brass voices. After the mid-1960s he became an international jazz ambassador, touring Europe as a soloist and living in Denmark briefly before returning to the US with wife Anne to continue starring at festivals and jazz parties as well as touring at home and abroad to order. Wild Bill's life and achievements are deservingly documented in a video produced by friend and fellow cornettist Tom Saunders, *Wild Bill Davison: His Life, His Time, His Music* (TT and T Network Inc, 1991), and in a biography, *The Wildest One*, by Hal Willard (Avondale, 1996).

Davison's solo discography is formidable too, but it is only very recently that his two principal masterpieces have been reissued by Arbors Records. The two albums (both with string orchestras) had their origins in a pair of tracks from Garry Moore's 1950s album *My Kind Of Music*, on which he teamed Davison with Percy Faith's orchestra ("a little like introducing Errol Flynn to a group from the YWCA!", Moore later recalled). The two titles ("Yesterdays" and "You Took Advantage Of Me") worked perfectly and led on to two more complete albums, **Pretty Wild** (with Faith again, and arrangements by Marty Manning, recorded in February 1956) and **With Strings Attached**, recorded eleven months later, with a Condon team of Dixieland premiers (plus Barry Galbraith on guitar) and strings arranged by Dean Kincaide. Both records are masterpieces, and such was the chagrin at their long-term deletion from catalogue that titles from both albums were re-recorded lock, stock and barrel for a new Davison LP in Copenhagen in 1976.

Now, however, the originals are back and they are still classics to treasure. *Pretty Wild* has his definitive retracing of Ellington's **Black Butterfly** and yearning almost rueful in **If I Had You**, as well as more jaunty outings on **Sugar** and **Mandy Make Up Your Mind**; there is also a **Wild Man Blues** comparable (though entirely different) to Armstrong's. On these tracks the levels of emotion that Davison conveys through his cornet are extraordinary, moving from brusque joy to the tenderness of a kiss. *With Strings Attached* perhaps lacks quite the emotional depth of its predecessor, but the cornettist once again excels throughout. "As soon as I played three bars," he said later of his *Pretty Wild* session, "I knew I had the shakes; a simple case of stage fright. So when I asked the conductor to send for a bottle of scotch whisky the tension broke right there!" Great art followed on, too – both times.

⮑We almost chose **Wild Bill Davison: The Commodore Master Takes**, GRP, 1997 [1943–45]

29

Vic Dickenson

Vic Dickenson Septet

Vanguard, 1993 (rec. 1953–54)

Dickenson (trombone), with Ruby Braff, Shad Collins (trumpet), Edmond Hall (clarinet), Sir Charles Thompson (piano), Steve Jordan (guitar), Walter Page (bass), Les Erskine, Jo Jones (drums).

The twelve titles on the **Vic Dickenson Septet** double CD – recorded over two days in December 1953 and November 1954, and originally issued as four separate 10" LPs – are historic for three reasons. Firstly, they provided quintessential confirmation (after almost thirty years) of the talents of trombonist Dickenson. Secondly, they prompted the invention (by Stanley Dance) of a new jazz category called "mainstream", in recognition that this music transcended current standard categories from "Dixieland" to "progressive", but in fact, for jazz-geographical purposes, stood somewhere between the two. Thirdly, and most importantly, they saw the glorious on-record emergence of a young trumpeter (later cornettist) instantly recognized, in the words of John Hammond's original sleevenotes, as "one of the great trumpeters of the day" – Ruby Braff.

Braff is now universally acknowledged as a grand master, but when these records first appeared he was a newcomer whose work at first hearing transformed the jazz world's vision of how a trumpet might sound. While not possessing Louis Armstrong's invincible strength (no one did), Braff presented a ravishing new view of Armstrong's approach, with delectable modifications of his own. Sensually lingering over phrases like a luxuriant lover (notably on a exploration of **I Cover The Waterfront**), setting strings of perfectly articulated high-speed runs against on-the-nose musical monosyllables (and never wasting a note either way), Braff delivered his solos with a tone that was bucket-deep, yet warm as a Yuletide fire, regularly exploring the trumpet's upper and (difficult) lower registers with coequal command. Around him Dickenson's sly avuncular witticisms and droll tonal trappings against Edmond Hall's more directly caustic yellow-toned clarinet not only furnished perfect ensemble support but regularly launched into solos which, without quite equalling Braff's brilliance, were powerful expositions of their own masters' strengths. Dickenson – like Dickie Wells and Bill Harris later – enjoyed the good-humoured aspect of the slide trombone; his contribution to **When You And I Were Young Maggie** is, in Hammond's words once again, "raucous, disrespectful and enormously stimulating". And the Basie-styled rhythm section behind the soloists – graced by the drums of Jo Jones and featuring the adaptable piano of "Sir" Charles Thompson – was a definition both of swing and the art of accompaniment.

The titles recorded in natural hall acoustics were long and luxurious; part of the contemporary acknowledgment that, now the LP was invented, jazz performers were at liberty to play for as long as they wanted. What's more remarkable still was that all the players sounded as if they are making full use of the space. On Braff's titles there is room to breathe between each phrase, and every solo is as considered and joyful a statement as a marriage proposal. Only trumpeter Shad Collins (a highly capable player who, after years with Count Basie, replaced Dizzy Gillespie with Cab Calloway in 1941) finds himself behind the eight ball in Braff's shadow. Collins' solos, while perfectly presentable, lack the breathtaking poise of the younger arrival. And his five tracks – including an agreeable **Nice Work If You Can Get It** and slightly anxious **Running Wild** (where his high-speed, cup-muted work sounds rather like someone trying to copy Braff) – cause the music, for the first time, to sound a little more like work than joyful, relaxed play. Braff, nevertheless – brought back as guest for a pair of tracks on session two – rehitches the music's wagon to his star, and within the bar all is well again.

⮑We almost chose **The Ruby Braff–George Barnes Quartet Live At The New School: The Complete Concert**, Chiaroscuro, undated [1974]

30

Eric Dolphy

Out To Lunch

Blue Note, 1987 (rec. 1964)

Dolphy (alto-sax, flute, bass-clarinet), Freddie Hubbard (trumpet), Bobby Hutcherson (vibraphone), Richard Davis (bass), Anthony Williams (drums).

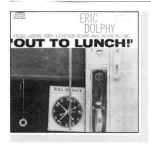

In the mid-1960s, the Blue Note label was known primarily as the headquarters of hard-bop, but the company also released some of the decade's most innovative, structurally challenging records. Jackie McLean, Sam Rivers, Grachan Moncur III, Cecil Taylor and Andrew Hill all issued forward-leaning records on the label. Eric Dolphy's **Out To Lunch** was the *pièce de resistance*, a session with such far-reaching compositional implications that they're still being grappled with today. It offered a relief from the conventionalization of hard-bop, suggesting new formal templates for jazz. And, for anyone under the misconception that freedom equals aimless flailing, here's just the liberated date to set you straight.

Dolphy's quintet for the studio session featured trumpeter Freddie Hubbard – a versatile post-bop mainstreamer who managed to be on three of the most important free-music recordings of the 1960s; here and on Ornette Coleman's *Free Jazz* and John Coltrane's *Ascension* – bassist Richard Davis, vibraphonist Bobby Hutcherson and a sensational eighteen-year-old drummer named Tony Williams. By that time, Williams had already made a splash as a member of the Miles Davis Quintet. In the context of Dolphy's music, his drumming was something altogether new – very open but very precise, with a taut, almost military snare sound, trademark light cymbals and tremendously creative hi-hat. But the most arresting thing was the way he used the drums as structural blocks, dropping out strategically, engaging with the front line directly, not simply supporting and accenting the flow. Hutcherson, too, ventures out front, adding ideas and textures rather than being a chord-comping piano substitute.

Dolphy's five original compositions provided a golden setting for this innovative play. As an alumnus of Mingus's great bands, he had the best role model possible in thinking about how to organize material, and the structuralist bent – setting up varied feels in one piece, working sectionally, creating dynamic backdrops for soloists – is evident throughout. On the opening theme to **Hat And Beard**, the members of the group take turns walking in 9/4 time, Williams providing countermotion with syncopated pings; Dolphy's bass-clarinet solo is searching, Hubbard a flutter of metallic motion, Hutcherson terse and considered over Davis's strummed ostinato and Williams's unthinkably inventive, restless brushes. Davis and Dolphy recorded alone together a year before (on *Music Matador*), and bass clarinet/bass duets bookend the ballad **Something Sweet, Something Tender**, displaying the full command Dolphy had on the bottom end of the long horn. Dedicated to contemporary classical flautist Severino Gazzelloni, **Gazzelloni** might make a believer of the most avowed flute-ophobe. Bright, chirpy and entirely consistent with his personal clarinet and sax vocabulary, Dolphy's is flute with none of the sappy or sentimental connotations. On this track, it's Williams's lithe bass-drum that astounds.

On the twelve-minute title track, Dolphy juxtaposes simple rhythmic elements to create a sophisticated collage-like piece with enormous implications, setting a stage for Anthony Braxton, Roscoe Mitchell, Anthony Davis and a host of other 1970s restructuralists. The melody to **Straight Up And Down** shows Dolphy's love of disjunction. Leaps from one register to another were integral to his alto playing, which is positively sparkling on this joyous, panoramic cut. Dolphy told A.B. Spellman: "Everyone's a leader in this session." While Dolphy still provided a compositional latticework, *Out To Lunch* made good on that claim, and it lives on as one of the real achievements of the post-bop period.

⮌We almost chose **At The Five Spot, Vol. 1**, OJC, 1992 [1961]

Duke Ellington

The Best Of Early Ellington

GRP, 1996 (rec. 1927–31)

Duke Ellington with his Kentucky Club Orchestra, The Washingtonians, Jungle Band, Cotton Club Orchestra, Hotsy-Totsy Gang, Orchestra. Principal soloists include Bubber Miley, Cootie Williams (trumpet), Tricky Sam Nanton (trombone), Barney Bigard (clarinet), Johnny Hodges (alto-sax), Harry Carney (baritone-sax) et al.

One of the most fascinating retrospective processes in jazz is to hear an artist developing through his recordings. This is easy with Duke Ellington (whose discography, like Louis Armstrong's, is formidable and consistent) and this CD covers the formative fifty-month period in which his orchestra transformed from junior "jungle jazz" beginnings into a fully mature ensemble which by 1931 could look ahead to Ellington's finest recording eras.

It was also a fascinating period in its own right. In 1923 Ellington and his young team had first moved from Washington to New York's thriving Harlem scene and found work at the Kentucky Club under banjoist Elmer Snowden. Ellington assumed leadership in 1924 (the year that the band began broadcasting) and new cornermen rapidly joined, including growl-trumpeter Bubber Miley and trombonist Charlie Irvis succeeded by Joe "Tricky Sam" Nanton. Johnny Hodges – who was to become one of jazz's three greatest altoists – arrived in 1928 (a year after Ellington profitably teamed with publisher Irving Mills) and Harry Carney joined the band in June 1927. Then on December 4, 1927 Ellington began his vital thirty-month season at the Cotton Club in Harlem, broadcasting from February to September 1929, for the mighty CBS network. It was now that his ensemble became national and soon international news, appearing in two movies (*Black And Tan Fantasy* and *Check*

And Double Check) for good measure, and by February 1931, after a five-month return to the Cotton Club, Duke Ellington and his orchestra were free to follow their star and did so.

From its first appearance in the studio for a major label in 1926, the orchestra produced classics. **East St. Louis Toodle-O** (electrically recorded and recognizably Ducal) announced his "arrival" both on record and – as his signature tune – on stage, until 1940. At this point Ellington's music sometimes sounds cartoon-esque and primitive (the repeated use of high clarinets, Miley's quivering plunger sound and even the odd fluff), but his scoring on early compositions like **Black And Tan Fantasy** (1927) was entirely original, and immensely ingenious. The creative development hereafter resembles the speeded-up film of a blossoming flower. By March 1928, **Jubilee Stomp** and the lyrical **Black Beauty** are sophisticated creations to set against Miley's vaudeville breaks on **Tishomingo Blues** or the Gothic horror of **The Mooche** from the same year. The beginnings of Ellington's unique voicings are already audible in **Yellow Dog Blues**, and soloists are developing too. Trombonist Tricky Sam Nanton seems to arrive ready-made; from June 1926 his central contributions track by track all demonstrate his tonal uniqueness. And Johnny Hodges is a particular joy. From early contributions on soprano saxophone, he can also be heard developing an assured alto voice as the CD progresses via "The Mooche", **Doin' The Voom-Voom** and finally **Creole Rhapsody**.

By early 1929 Miley has been replaced by Cootie Williams whose open-trumpet strength and command of the plunger are heard on **Jolly Wog** and **Jazz Convulsions** respectively; by this second track Carney has found his way to the baritone chair, too. Then in October 1930 comes the immortal **Mood Indigo** (the clarinet part scored a full octave lower than the brass) and by January 14, 1931 and **Rockin' In Rhythm**, everything is in place; any latterday Ellington fan could sing this arrangement note for note. One last track – the two-part "Creole Rhapsody" – is the perfect sign-off. Ellington's first extended composition displays all his mature dignities and the cartoons in the music have gone forever.

⮑No alternative **– an incomparable selection**

Duke Ellington

The Blanton-Webster Band

RCA/Bluebird, 1986 (rec. 1940–42)

Ellington (piano), Wallace Jones, Cootie Williams (trumpet), Rex Stewart (cornet),
Tricky Sam Nanton, Lawrence Brown (trombone), Juan Tizol (valve-trombone),
Barney Bigard, Johnny Hodges, Otto Hardwick, Ben Webster, Harry Carney (reeds),
Billy Strayhorn (piano), Fred Guy (guitar), Jimmy Blanton (bass), Sonny Greer
(drums), Ivy Anderson, Herb Jeffries (vocals).

Like Louis Armstrong (his principal contender for artistic supremacy in twentieth-century American jazz), Duke Ellington's musical development is fulsomely represented in discographical terms. Amid the cornucopia there are regular zeniths (as well as the odd nadir) spread over five decades. But many of his most devoted – and informed – admirers regularly cite the music of **The Blanton–Webster Band** as Ellington's finest on record.

The dual presence of Blanton and Webster is a benchmark rather than *raison d'être* for the music's excellence. Ben Webster was already a premier tenor-saxophone soloist by the time he rejoined Ellington's band in January 1940; the phenomenal double-bassist Jimmy Blanton, who had arrived a few months previously (and who left the band in 1941 prior to death from tuberculosis at only 23), is acknowledged by later masters such as Ray Brown as the father of contemporary methodology for his instrument. Both men were willingly lending their talents to Ellington at a crucial creative high point in his own career; an artistic partnership with Billy Strayhorn was beginning after fourteen years in which Ellington's orchestra had moved on from "jungle music" through a 1930s decade of technical and artistic expansion (including his extended compositions, beginning with "Creole Rhapsody" in 1931). By 1940 it seemed as if Duke, his new amanuensis and his orchestra were all standing like pipers at the gates of a great creative dawn.

By 1940 virtually every player in Ellington's orchestra was a major voice bound for jazz immortality. And the same thing could be said for many of the 66 recordings fashioned by Ellington and Strayhorn in the 29 months between March 1940 and July 1942. Within one year a succession of masterpieces conceived by the leader alone – **Ko-Ko**, **Morning Glory**, **Concerto For Cootie**, **Bojangles**, **Sepia Panorama** and more – had flooded from the instrument which was his orchestra. It didn't seem to matter that in 1941 – an ASCAP ban temporarily barred much previously written popular music from the radio waves – Ellington (shored up by significant writing support from Strayhorn as well as son Mercer and valve-trombonist Juan Tizol) continued to ride his wave. It was only the full-time ban on recording by James C. Petrillo's American Federation of Musicians that finally stopped the story until December 1944.

If Ellington had never recorded again, however, his immortality would be assured with the music here. Track by track it offers supreme demonstrations of his compositional genius; of the total originality with which he used the instrumental possibilities of a dance orchestra and, of course, the uncanny creative unity cemented between Ellington and Strayhorn (in later years it was frequently impossible to be sure who had composed what). Classic examples here include Strayhorn's own **Take The "A" Train** (Ellington's signature tune from 1941), **Raincheck**, and the almost spectral **Chelsea Bridge**. Ellington's myriad classics (including three random examples – the tone poem **Harlem Air Shaft**, echoingly impressionistic "Sepia Panorama" and stunning, menacing "Ko-Ko") were instantly to take their place among his most revered work. And even less profound diversions (**At A Dixie Roadside Diner**, **Hayfoot Strawfoot** and **A Slip Of The Lip (Can Sink A Ship)**) are still irresistible. Classic solos also abound – Nance on "Take The 'A' Train", Webster's roughhouse tenor on **Cottontail** and Blanton's nimble bass on "Ko-Ko".

⊃No alternative – **this is a complete set**

33

Duke Ellington

Ellington At Newport 1956 (Complete)

Columbia Legacy, 1999 (rec. 1956)

Ellington (piano), Cat Anderson, Willie Cook, Ray Nance, Clark Terry (trumpets),
Quentin Jackson, Britt Woodman (trombones), John Sanders (valve-trombone),
Jimmy Hamilton, Johnny Hodges, Russell Procope, Paul Gonsalves, Harry Carney
(reeds), Jimmy Woode (bass), Sam Woodyard (drums).

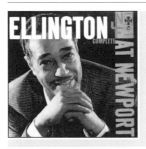

By 1956 Duke Ellington's orchestra had been in recorded existence for three decades, surviving both the fast-forward changes in jazz fashion that were still in full flight and the final decline of big bands amid the importunate arrival of rock'n'roll. The early 1950s had not, on the face of it, treated Ellington kindly. The divine musical focuses of the Blanton–Webster era had seemingly dissipated postwar; key cornermen including Sonny Greer, Lawrence Brown and, most damagingly, Johnny Hodges had left his orchestra in 1951, and in the next few years Ellington's output for Capitol Records – including titles like "Bunny Hop Mambo" – seemed somehow disturbed and compromised.

All this was to be changed definitively with the issue of **Ellington At Newport 1956** – a live concert which had literally caused a riot and which, once and for all, would reinstate Ellington as first lord of the jazz orchestra. It also appeared to herald the reopening of his creative floodgates, and an era which would produce a string of new and recharged recorded masterpieces; *A Drum Is A Woman, Such Sweet Thunder, Anatomy Of A Murder, Piano In the Background, Nutcracker Suite, Peer Gynt Suite* and more – all of them required listening for any serious Ellington student.

Ellington At Newport was his all-time bestseller, nevertheless. It achieved this, above all, for a performance which has entered the halls of jazz legend (and which created the commotion) – **Diminuendo And Crescendo In Blue**. This two-part composition, originally recorded by Ellington's orchestra in 1937, had stayed in his book ever since and sometime during 1951 had been replayed at Birdland, acquiring in the process an ad hoc interlude, based on the blues, from tenorist Paul Gonsalves. Five years later, Ellington repeated the format at Newport; Gonsalves played 27 straight choruses to an audience already ecstatically on its feet and who soon began dancing. At the end of the performance there was pandemonium, and once again Ellington was front-page news.

The album that followed this sensational evening had troubles of its own. Gonsalves had mistakenly directed his historic solo towards a second microphone set up for the Voice of America broadcasting system, rather than Columbia Records. Consequently, on record, it delivered less impact, prompting a legacy of studio re-recording, editing and dubbing by the great producer George Avakian, before the finished 12" LP was released for public hearing. When it materialized – comprising a classic replay of **Jeep's Blues** by the luminous Hodges, plus a striking three-part **Newport Jazz Festival Suite** and concluding with the audible (and occasionally enhanced) riot which accompanied "Diminuendo And Crescendo" – Avakian had created another classic which is still one of jazz's greatest on-record moments, over forty years on.

Some listeners may wish to hear it first, too. But, in addition to the original studio-adjusted album material, this CD reissue offers numerous bonuses, including the original concert in its entirety and as performed. There are bonus tracks (from both the concert and studio recordings) and, triumphantly, Columbia's tapes have been combined with newly traced Voice of America masters to restore Gonsalves' legendary solo to full power, creating authentic stereo into the bargain. Producer Phil Schaap tells the whole story in a definitive commentary that offers explanations as well as posing the odd artistic conundrum. But, in the end, all of this great music is its own message.

⊃We almost chose **Such Sweet Thunder**, Columbia Legacy, 1999 [1956–57]

34

Bill Evans

Waltz For Debby

OJC, 1987 (rec. 1961)

Evans (piano), Scott LaFaro (bass), Paul Motian (drums).

Evans is revered for his pivotal contribution to the distinctive sound of Miles Davis's *Kind Of Blue*. His touch on the acoustic keyboard was only one of the things Davis praised, and crucial to their brief collaboration was the fact that Evans was interested in modal improvisation not dictated by the underlying chords. Influenced in this direction during an association with the composer-thinker George Russell, Bill had many other things going for him – a deep understanding and affinity for harmony (born of studying classical and twentieth-century piano literature), an enviable technique capable of spinning long lines reminiscent of the ascetic Lennie Tristano, plus a rhythmic suppleness and flexibility quite foreign to Tristano.

Only known to a few before joining Miles, Evans was afterwards able to start his first regular trio. In short order, he became the most influential pianist since Bud Powell a decade-and-a-half earlier, having a marked effect on subsequent newcomers such as Herbie Hancock, Chick Corea, Keith Jarrett and even McCoy Tyner (whereas the impact of his contemporary Cecil Taylor took far longer to be absorbed by others). While Evans's interests were remote from the further reaches of free jazz, his partnership with bassist Scott LaFaro and drummer Paul Motian was significant in helping rhythm-sections move beyond the tight togetherness of hard-bop towards the Hancock – Ron Carter – Tony Williams flexibility of Miles's mid-1960s quintet.

The trio had set down two astonishing studio albums, *Portrait In Jazz* and *Exploration*, in the eighteen months preceding this live date at New York's Village Vanguard. The interplay ("collective improvisation" is a better description) between Evans and LaFaro draws the ear to the group's innovative stance, though it's the varied responses of Motian (from the minimal to the subtly aggressive) that make it work. LaFaro drew on advances already established by Paul Chambers and by Mingus but, equally clearly, he thought along the same lines as Evans – often imitating or (on **Detour Ahead**) anticipating his phrases – while his freedom when indicating harmonic roots (and routes) extended to a frequent refusal to mark the first beat of the bar. In his own solos he plays around with the beat just like Charlie Parker, for instance opening his chorus on **My Romance** by quoting the tune but doing it late and threatening to throw off his colleagues.

Evans still dominates the proceedings, and often in the most understated way. This is particularly noticeable in the magical ballads which, despite the background noise on some other tracks, obviously held the audience spellbound (the exception is **Porgy**, initially unreleased, though you're unlikely to notice the distant interruption on a second hearing). The positive effects of working live are noticeable everywhere, including these first trio versions of the famous title track, "My Romance" and **Some Other Time**, tunes which Bill had previously done unaccompanied – he had also used the introduction of the last-named as a basis for his "Peace Piece" and for Miles Davis's "Flamenco Sketches".

Another live moment follows the theme on the first version of "Detour Ahead", where (just as on *Kind Of Blue*'s "Blue In Green") Evans doubles the harmonic rhythm, audibly taking LaFaro by surprise. A mere ten days later, the bassist died in a car crash aged 25 – the same age as Clifford Brown when he met a similar fate – which adds to the value of these recordings. But you hardly need to know about this, or about Evans's up-and-down career thereafter, in order to be moved by the music.

●We almost chose **Conversations With Myself**, Verve, 1997 [1963]

35

Ella Fitzgerald

For The Love Of Ella

Verve, 1989 (rec. 1956–66)

Ella Fitzgerald, with Jazz At The Philharmonic, Paul Smith's Quartot, Marty Paich's Orchestra, Duke Ellington's Orchestra, Count Basie's Orchestra/Octet, Nelson Riddle's Orchestra, Roy Eldridge, Louis Armstrong, Ben Webster (trumpet), Stuff Smith (tenor-sax), Barney Kessel (violin), Billy May's Orchestra, Oscar Peterson, Buddy Bregman's Orchestra.

In the regularly confusing world of jazz, arguments have raged for years over who is, or isn't, a jazz singer. The problem is that, so far, no one has managed to define exactly what jazz is. If improvisation is the keyword, then what happens to the towering written-down creations of Duke Ellington or Gil Evans? Either way, singers – who are principally in the different business of song interpretation anyhow – tend to fade in and out of focus depending on their surroundings. Frank Sinatra – apparently a jazz singer when with the Metronome All Stars – stops being one with Axel Stordahl's strings; now you hear him, now you don't.

Ella Fitzgerald, however, had both bases covered. An inspired and near-incomparable scat singer (encouraged to improvise by Dizzy Gillespie), she was plainly a grade-A improviser as well as the most poised and universally acknowledged female popular singer of the twentieth century. Her songbook albums – recorded for Norman Granz between 1956 and 1964, and celebrating Porter, Rodgers and Hart, Ellington, Berlin, Gershwin, Arlen, Kern and Mercer – set both her artistry and her material in deserving definitive surroundings, transformed her finally from ingénue to diva, and are classics for joyous exploration. But, for some listeners accustomed to the hard stuff of jazz rather than the glories of

American popular song, they may not belong in this book.

So, with the humble recommendation that jazz is where you find it, on to **For The Love Of Ella**, in which her jazz credentials are constantly and joyously on show almost throughout. Fitzgerald always seemed entirely comfortable in the company of jazz musicians as, of course, she had been since childhood, when her guardian was her bandleader, too – the incomparable drummer Chick Webb. With Webb, Fitzgerald set irreproachable standards for swing-singing. Her recording partners in the 1940s included Louis Armstrong, Louis Jordan, the Delta Rhythm Boys, Ink Spots and the Mills Brothers, and from 1947 two recorded scat-outings "Flying Home" and **Lady Be Good** established her as an adventurous jazz improviser. From 1949 she starred with Granz's Jazz At The Philharmonic touring show and from 1956 recorded more hit albums with Armstrong – informal meetings with an old friend which contrast wonderfully with her songbooks.

For The Love Of Ella celebrates Fitzgerald's best jazz years. From 1957, at the Shrine Auditorium, Los Angeles, there are two classic scat extravaganzas, ("Lady Be Good" and **Stompin' At The Savoy**) with the whole JATP team, and four more from the incomparable *Ella In Berlin* album from 1960, with pianist Paul Smith's quartet. Set alongside such superlative live titles are similar five-star studio cuts including four tracks from her Ellington songbook (with Ellington's orchestra and a small group featuring Ben Webster and violinist Stuff Smith), two with Louis Armstrong and Oscar Peterson's quartet from 1957, and titles with Count Basie's orchestra and octet featuring Joe Williams on the irresistible **Party Blues**. Other beauties here include a pair of tracks from the great 1963 album *These Are The Blues* (featuring trumpeter Roy Eldridge and organist Wild Bill Davis) and, as a bonus, five tracks from the Gershwin, Mercer and Arlen songbook collections. Devotees of "dinner-jazz" will no doubt appreciate this otherwise irreproachable double CD's division into "Monuments of Swing" and "Ballads and blues", but please don't clink the cutlery.

➲We almost chose **Sings The Rodgers & Hart Song Book,**

Verve, 1997 [1956]

36

Bill Frisell

This Land

Elektra Nonesuch, 1994 (rec. 1992)

Frisell (guitar), Curtis Fowlkes (trombone), Don Byron (clarinet, bass clarinet), Billy Drewes (alto-sax), Kermit Driscoll (bass, electric bass), Joey Baron (drums).

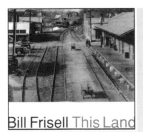

Bill Frisell This Land

Bill Frisell's approach comes across as an extraordinarily effective blend of cool jazz and wild rock. He studied under Jim Hall, who was his idol and whose meticulous deployment of space clearly got through. Since then, he has incorporated many sound effects linked to rock stars and added his own, forming the aptly named Power Tools (a high-octane trio with electric bassist Melvin Gibbs and drummer Ronald Shannon Jackson) and being part of John Zorn projects. But flashy runs and ear-crunching power for its own sake are out. Even when decibels boil over, he aims above all to create a tonal landscape and there is often a sense of lazy, country-style picking, perhaps the legacy of years spent growing up in Colorado.

That side of him dominates the groups he has led during the past decade, landscapes evoked being those of the country blues. The opening tracks here, up to and including the title tune, could be described as closely argued mood pieces, carefully arranged by Frisell but giving ensemble members leeway. They contribute equally to the overall texture, while his bent notes, whining chords and heavy guitar licks make all the more impact for being deployed so meticulously. **Jimmy Carter (Part 2)** works out as a sort of mini-concerto for the dancing drum patterns of Joey Baron. **Is It Sweet?** revolves around a duet between guitar and bass-clarinet and **This Land** produces an eerie clash between atmospheric guitar and repeated ensemble figures.

The front-line members of his sextet are all identified with the sharp end of jazz improvisation, and they have longer spells in the foreground on the remaining pieces. Bringing to the trombone a strong high register and an acute understanding of the instrument's capacity for the rasps, wheezes and slurs that have engrossed us since the heyday of Tricky Sam Nanton, Curtis Fowlkes struts his stuff most notably as he interweaves with the ensemble on **Dog Eats Dog** – the slightly sinister theme, when it appears, reminds one of Carla Bley and could slot easily into *Escalator Over The Hill*.

Frisell's groups from this period usually include Don Byron, a clarinettist whose agitated, decidedly city-wise lines provide the ideal contrast with his own. Often taking the high-note lead in the ensembles, he and Frisell blend superbly during a call-and-response passage on **Julius Hemphill**. The longest track on the album, it inches at a stately pace to a remarkable conclusion, the theme rising an octave while Frisell strums and billows below. A soloist in the style of Arthur Blythe, Billy Drewes contributes a slightly sweet sound to the mix and is well suited to the Caribbean lilt of **Amarillo Barbados**.

If the album's immediately identifiable impact derives from the group sound, the material varies considerably track by track. As its name implies, **Rag** is pastiche ragtime, very well done and something of a Frisell hit which he had previously recorded on his 1989 Nonesuch album *Is That You*. The swing-band melody of **Monica Jane** gets treated appropriately – except, of course, for Frisell's subversive colours splayed over the top, while the slinky tempo and rocking bass-lines from Kermit Driscoll inspire a selection of the guitarist's whinnying chords, firmly in the blues tradition. Somewhat camouflaged, the twelve-bar blues itself turns up on **Resistor**, its bebop-type theme carried by hip-hop rhythms as Byron, Drewes and Frisell reach their optimum solo levels.

➲We almost chose **Quartet**, Elektra, 1996

37

Jan Garbarek

Twelve Moons

ECM, 1993 (rec. 1992)

Garbarek (soprano-sax, tenor-sax, synth), Rainer Brüninghaus (piano, synth),
Eberhard Weber (bass), Manu Katché (drums), Marilyn Mazur (percussion), Agnes
Buen Garnås, Mari Boine (vocals).

The contribution of Norwegian saxophonist Jan Garbarek is a dramatic illustration of one way that jazz has developed in recent decades. Twenty years old when Coltrane died, he had already appeared on record (with singer Karin Krog) as a talented follower of Trane's middle-period music, and soon added the influence of Albert Ayler and other free-jazz saxists. But the long-term presence in Scandinavia of Don Cherry and composer George Russell – a reminder that not only mainstream US artists felt the need to emigrate in the second half of the 1960s – was crucial in drawing out the characteristics of several local musicians.

Russell (under whom Garbarek studied as well as performed) had an important influence on the saxophonist's compositional urge, but Cherry (with whom he worked far less) was crucially engaged in learning lessons from the foreigners he played with, whether jazz-inclined or more ethnic performers. His inspiration led many acolytes to investigate for themselves the beauties of folk-music of all kinds, and it's perhaps no coincidence that one of Garbarek's early albums (co-led by Swedish pianist Bobo Stenson) was named after the song "Witchi-Tai-To", a Native American chant introduced to the jazz field by Don Cherry sideman Jim Pepper. While his work with Keith Jarrett's European quartet of the mid to late 1970s brought Garbarek closer to the jazz mainstream, it was his own personal development that led to his present eminence.

During what is now a thirty-year association with ECM, Garbarek has not only come to personify many of the qualities and aims of the label, but has gained hugely from the freedom it has given him. Part of this process has consisted of opening himself to the ethnic music of northern Europe, an explicit element of **Twelve Moons** and an important factor in several earlier albums. Garbarek's progress is also shown by the gradual individuation of his coolly sensuous saxophone tone, which is instantly identifiable and often conjures up images of stark natural landscapes. ECM's distinctive cover art invites this kind of interpretation, but it's the grandeur of his playing and the simplicity of his musical materials that count.

In an artfully arranged programme, the album begins at its most middle-of-the-road, with a title suite composed for the film *Around The Year In Borfjord* featuring Garbarek's soprano and synth accompanied only by ethnic-sounding percussion. Track two being a traditional **Psalm** (one of the two items to include a female vocalist, here Agnes Buen Garnås), the full instrumental quintet is not heard until track four, and it's not till the following piece that a jazz feel dominates, coinciding with the leader's first use of the tenor. Now also the sound of Eberhard Weber (a bandleader in his own right and an international influence on the fretless bass) becomes more prominent, as it is on the succeeding **Arietta**, written by Garbarek's composer compatriot, Edvard Grieg.

The Bill Evans/Keith Jarrett inheritance of Brüninghaus's acoustic piano is heard here and notably on **Huhai**, which quotes from Sami folk-sources. But the most extraordinary piece on the record is perhaps the unaccompanied duet between singer Mari Boine and Garbarek's tenor, which (to mix geographical metaphors) sounds like an alp-horn. The self-referential, hermetic nature of this bewitching musical universe is underlined by a reprise of **Brother Wind March** from the 1988 album *Legend Of The Seven Dreams,* and indeed by a new **Witchi-Tai-To** that's far more individual than the saxophonist's 1973 version.

⮑We almost chose **I Took Up The Runes**, ECM, 1991 [1990]

38

Erroll Garner

Concert By The Sea

Columbia, 1987 (rec. 1955)

Garner (piano), Eddie Calhoun (bass), Denzil Best (drums).

Garner was a maverick in a field not short of such phenomena, especially in its earlier days. A diminutive figure with a puckish sense of musical humour, he was nicknamed "The Elf" by his colleagues and played in a way that was unique for his time, or any other. It's perfectly possible to find him less than essential, on the ground that a schematic view of jazz history has no useful pigeonhole for him (but, fifty years ago, they were saying the same thing about Duke Ellington!). Nevertheless, even the most hardhearted or academically minded observers are liable to be won over by Garner's captivating performance.

The most obvious facet of his style, and at faster tempos the most compelling, is the independence of his hands. Garner is always doing different things at the same time, with the left hand spelling out four beats to the bar like a swing-era rhythm guitarist, while also using isolated low notes in the manner of a drummer "dropping bombs" (accenting) on his bass-drum. All this provides such a strong foundation that his right hand is then able to lag tantalizingly behind the established beat, whether playing complex single-note improvisations or huge big-band-style chords. Elements of his approach can be traced to the influence of the great Earl Hines, who grew up in the same town of Pittsburgh and was becoming widely known through records and radio when Erroll was still a precocious child star.

Garner's compelling one-man band reduces the roles of bassist and drummer to a gentle whisper of accompaniment, with which he often dispensed, as in the opening choruses of **April In Paris** and **Autumn Leaves**, but the presence of an audience on the present album is more significant. The pianist's changes of dynamics and direction evoke their almost tangible delight (matched by his own occasional Lionel Hampton-ish grunts between phrases), which becomes explicit in the outright applause greeting the end of his audacious introductions as a familiar tune abruptly heaves into view. Examples are heard on, for instance, **Where Or When** and **I'll Remember April**, which, like much else in the programme, were already well-worn standards vividly brought to new life by the pianist's treatment.

It's worth noting, though, that "Autumn Leaves" was a relatively new tune to the US and, even more so, Cole Porter's **It's All Right With Me** and Sammy Cahn's **Teach Me Tonight**, indicating that Garner took his role as an entertainer just as seriously as performers of the preceding Hines/Armstrong generation. Equally clear is his commitment to lesser-known colleagues within the jazz world, as shown by the inclusion of Gene Ammons's recent r&b hit **Red Top** and Tyree Glenn's **How Could You Do A Thing Like That To Me**. Apart from the brief closing theme, Erroll's only original is the fast **Mambo Carmel**, during the Latin portions of which his left hand switches effortlessly to a clave rhythm, as indeed it does in parts of "Where Or When".

It was quite fortuitous that this live recording was released at all, but its success (as one of the bestselling piano records of all time) helped Garner's growing reputation, to the extent that he was soon working internationally for a leading classical-music impresario. A year earlier he had created the standard "Misty" (recorded on *Contrasts*), which further assisted his bank balance, but it was his ebullient piano work that made him the most widely popular jazz musician of his generation.

⮑ We almost chose **Contrasts**, Verve, 1998 [1954]

39

Stan Getz

At The Opera House

Verve, 1986 (rec. 1957)

Getz (tenor-sax), J.J. Johnson (trombone), Oscar Peterson (piano), Herb Ellis (guitar), Ray Brown (bass), Connie Kay, Louis Bellson (drums).

Stan Getz has long been one of the most genuinely popular of jazz musicians. The several reasons for this include an unfailing sense of melody, reflecting the influence of both Lester Young and European music. Getz had an unashamedly seductive saxophone tone or, rather, a whole series of different tones at different stages of his career, each seeming just right for the period. Also communicating subtly to the average listener is his understated but precise rhythmic alertness.

There's a lot of Getz on record, and perhaps a majority of his albums feature just his saxophone and a rhythm-section, the earliest ones establishing his reputation for sighing ballads and frothy uptempos. His 1950s live sessions (*At Storyville*, *At The Shrine* and the present choice, **At The Opera House**) and later 1950s studio sets (such as *West Coast Jazz*) show Getz flexing his muscles. In the 1960s, a famous suite with strings (*Focus*) summarized his achievement to date, while his bossanova hits only engaged part of his attention. By the end of the decade, he was semi-retired but in the 1970s he adopted a wide variety of settings, while the 1980s brought a final distillation of his art. His last studio album in 1990 found him bolstered by synthesizers.

No wonder that tenor colleague Zoot Sims memorably called Getz "a nice bunch of guys", although he was probably referring to personality as much as music. Ironically, the chosen album finds Stan at his most Zoot-like, with an ability to swing at the drop of a hat while creating melodic gems. Having another horn often brought out the best in Getz, for instance, with Bob Brookmeyer and on three different occasions Chet Baker. Teamed for a 1957 Jazz At The Philharmonic tour with a relative stranger, J.J. Johnson (who'd also had a similar partnership with fellow trombonist Kai Winding), he was recorded on two separate nights, once for an early stereo album and once for the then-dominant mono format. The CD reissue, jointly billed as by Getz and Johnson, contains almost all of the two original albums.

The majority of the material is simple, standard material such as two fastish blues, Charlie Parker's **Billie's Bounce** and Oscar Pettiford's **Blues In The Closet**, and the (respectively) 1920s and 1930s songs, **Crazy Rhythm** and **My Funny Valentine**. Even the latter is removed from its typical jazz-ballad treatment for a rhythmic romp that finds Getz, especially in the mono version, occasionally roughing up his tone and dishing out high-register staccato notes as if swishing a sword through the air. Johnson, who like Getz was also turning out a series of superior studio albums at this period, was moving towards a more melodically mellow style, as shown in his feature with just the rhythm-section, the medium-tempo **Yesterdays**. The only ballad is the one track without Johnson, an economically phrased, emotively articulated one-and-a-half choruses of **It Never Entered My Mind**.

The mono concert may be the more cohesive one and the balance is certainly more compact – unconnected with this, it seems Louis Bellson is the stereo drummer rather than the advertised Kay. Except for introductions, Peterson (who filled this role countless times on JATP tours and studio sessions) is heard only in the rhythm-section, with the two horns hogging all the solo space. Though no one album or even a successful compilation could give the whole of Getz, this is a part that should not be forgotten.

⮌We almost chose **Focus**, Verve, 1997 [1961]

40

Dizzy Gillespie

The Complete RCA Victor Recordings

RCA Victor, 1995 (rec. 1937–49)

Gillespie (trumpet, vocals), with Teddy Hill and Lionel Hampton Orchestras and Metronome All Stars, and own bands including Don Byas, James Moody (tenor-sax), Al Haig, John Lewis (piano), Milt Jackson (vibraphone), Ray Brown (bass), Kenny Clarke (drums).

In an interesting parallel with Louis Armstrong, Gillespie's music was overtaken later in life by his outsize personality, his corny jokes and even some singing. But, whereas Louis's vocal work was one of his important pioneering contributions, Dizzy was pre-eminently a trumpeter and, not insignificantly, an arranger-composer, too. He was perhaps also more of a true band-leader for, while musicians played as well they could with Louis out of sheer reverence, Gillespie was able to whip his men into shape musically. On the trumpet, what seemed at first like wilfully weird phrasing (here there's a parallel with his colleague Thelonious Monk) was backed up with an exact theoretical knowledge.

The early work indeed stands out triumphantly against the backdrop of jazz history, and this two-CD set includes his first recorded solos. Three tracks, from 1937 (when he was only nineteen) show him preoccupied with imitating his idol, Roy Eldridge, who two years earlier had made his name with the same bandleader (Teddy Hill). The single Gillespie solo with Hampton's impressively all-star studio group finds the trumpeter in 1939 already moving on from Roy. A leap to 1946 brings us the fully formed leader of the bebop school, exploring the link between straight time and Afro-Cuban rhythms. Diz's **Night In Tunisia**, already performed with the Earl Hines, Billy Eckstine and Boyd Raeburn big bands, appears in his own first version with the 1946 small group in which Don Byas had recently replaced Charlie Parker (who does, however, appear on four 1949 Metronome All Stars tracks).

Some of Gillespie's earliest sides with Parker are collected on *Groovin' High* (Savoy), but by the mid-1940s he'd spent nearly a decade playing in and arranging for other people's big bands, and the sound attracted him enough for him to form his own in 1946. Its work constitutes the bulk of this collection and, as well as displaying an intriguing compromise between the vitality of small-group bebop and the power of a large ensemble, it also extends Dizzy's love affair with Afro-Cuban music. His collaboration with the *conguero* Chano Pozo enlivens eight tracks from 1947, with other percussionists stepping in after Pozo's untimely death. Among these items are **Algo Bueno** (a rewrite of Gillespie's earlier "Woody'n You" for Mr Herman), **Guarachi Guaro** (later a hit for Cal Tjader, retitled "Soul Sauce"), the famous **Manteca** and the futuristic **Cubana Be-Cubana Bop**, co-written by Dizzy and George Russell.

The rest of the album features more straight-ahead big-band music spiced by typical bop melody lines, arranged by Tadd Dameron and others, plus Gillespie's approach to scat-singing on **Ool-Ya-Koo** and **Oop-Pop-A-Da**. Ironically, by 1949 he was making accommodations with the newly popular rhythm-and-blues style and occasionally tailoring his trumpet style for more simplistic ears. But there was much fine music still to come, including that of another big band in 1956–57, which can be heard on *Birks Works* (Verve), and a famous Massey Hall concert appearance discussed under Charlie Parker. Meanwhile, the trumpet innovations heard here had an unmistakable influence on all who followed, while his combination of bebop and swing conventions became standard for future big-band ventures. His first successful Afro-Cuban ventures were a defining moment for the development of Latin jazz and, as a further spin-off of this band, the last four names listed among the sidemen constituted the first edition of what became the Modern Jazz Quartet.

⊃We almost chose **Diz 'N Bird At Carnegie Hall**, Blue Note, 1997 [1947]

41

Jimmy Giuffre

The Jimmy Giuffre 3

Atlantic, 1988 (rec. 1956–57)

Giuffre (tenor-sax, baritone-sax, clarinet), Jim Hall (guitar), Ralph Pena, Jim Atlas (bass),

Towards the end of the 1940s, the name of Jimmy Giuffre meant first and foremost the talented composer of "Four Brothers", the Woody Herman hit that launched Stan Getz. By the end of the 1950s, it connoted a fellow saxophonist who led an unconventional trio, such as the one on this album and the one seen in the film *Jazz On A Summer's Day*. (The name, incidentally, is pronounced "Joo-fri" and not any of the variants created particularly by British speakers.) By the early 1960s, however, he had espoused a radical form of free-jazz (heard on the reissue *1961*) that found few takers at the time and reduced him, a decade further on, to college teaching for a living.

There is a sense, however, in which these various activities are not as far apart as they may seem. Giuffre's arranging, and the soloists he wrote for in the Herman band, were all inspired by Lester Young, whose innovations on both the tenor sax and clarinet (perhaps Jimmy's most important instrument) were clearly the strongest influence on his 1950s playing. The examples here, though ostensibly based on straight forward diatonic harmonies, also remind the listener that Young's relative unconcern for chord sequences and his paramount interest in the melodic line (even when it was fairly a-melodic) pointed directly towards modal and free playing.

Though little of the music here is out of tempo, the relaxation arising from the then-revolutionary absence of drums makes collective improvisation easier to achieve. While Giuffre's playing, both on his own material and a couple of unhackneyed standards, is relatively simple and subdued, the young Jim Hall (fresh from his debut with Chico Hamilton) is tremendously responsive and versatile, his guitar filling in for another saxophone or a trumpet, or even for drums, as required. The leader's writing taps into a vein of folk music, and even at times country music, that was new to jazz and, in the pastoral melodies of the long but varied **Crawdad Suite**, creates a sense of spaciousness unique at the time.

The highlight of the set, **The Train And The River**, summarizes all these virtues and, whether or not it's intended to be taken programmatically, the opening section is in an even 8/8, contrasting with the swing feel of the second theme. (The opening also is in the same key and has a slightly similar feel to Ornette Coleman's "Ramblin'", which came along three years later.) Two bonus tracks from the following year, including **The Green Country (New England Mood)**, have Atlas replacing Pena on bass but were subsequently re-recorded with Giuffre's new trio of himself, Hall and valve-trombonist Bob Brookmeyer. This is the group that played "The Train And The River" in the famous opening sequence of *Jazz On A Summer's Day* but, with the live CD of that performance (*Hollywood And Newport, 1957–58*) seemingly out of print, the piece's studio premiere remains a significant landmark.

This "folk-jazz", as it was already being called at the time, was met with derision by some, who felt it was lacking the guts of either genuine folk music or indeed truly earthy jazz. What they would make of the sort of ethnic borrowings that have infected much contemporary jazz, especially coming from Europe, is anyone's guess. But it's fair to say that it was Giuffre who opened up the form and made such developments possible. It's also fair to say that the present album is not only historically important but very easy on the ear.

⟳We almost chose **1961**, ECM, 1992 [1961]

42

Benny Goodman

The Famous 1938 Carnegie Hall Jazz Concert

Columbia Legacy, 1999

Goodman (clarinet, leader), with Harry James, Ziggy Elman, Chris Griffin (trumpet), Rod Ballard, Vernon Brown (trombone), Hymie Schertzer, George Koenig, Art Rollini, Babe Russin (reeds), Jess Stacy (piano), Allan Reuss (guitar), Harry Goodman (bass), Gene Krupa (drums), Martha Tilton, Goodman (vocals).

From the moment that Benny Goodman in huntsman's tails took the stage at Carnegie Hall on a chilly January evening in 1938, it was plain that jazz was in for a night to remember. By now Goodman was already dubbed "The King of Swing" via his hit radio broadcasts for Camel Caravan, and it was Wynn Nathanson, a representative of the programmes, who first conceived the idea of the concert. New York's Acolian Hall had already played host to an equally historic concert (by Paul Whiteman) fourteen years previously, but the idea of swing music in New York's principal classical bastion was still revolutionary and this team of youthful swing firebrands were well aware of the challenges inherent in the concept. Goodman prepared his programme cannily, combining proven band set pieces with one or two fresh selections plus items from his trio and quartet. And as a precaution allied talent was called in, including stars from the Count Basie and Duke Ellington orchestras.

The triumphant result, from Goodman's opening downbeat on **Don't Be That Way**, was a concert whose central position in jazz history was reconfirmed after its issue in edited form on LP by Columbia in 1950. Most of the evening's music was retained, including peak-level performances from Goodman's ensembles, an extended (but edited) jam session on **Honeysuckle Rose** –

also featuring Lester Young, Buck Clayton, Johnny Hodges, Count Basie, Freddie Green and Walter Page – and a worthy retrospective **Twenty Years Of Jazz** conceived by Irving Kolodin (whose fine liner notes are retained on this issue) featuring the visiting Ellingtonians (their leader was in the wings) and cornettist Bobby Hackett, saluting Bix Beiderbecke. This two-volume LP set has long been a landmark in jazz discography, and listeners from that generation have got used to accepting its contents as the full record of an unforgettable jazz evening.

This CD issue, however – produced to the highest artistic and aesthetic standards by multi-Grammy award-winning producer Phil Schaap – corrects the on-record modifications of the evening by presenting the concert exactly as it happened in real time, including walk-ons, pauses for setting up and, of course, applause. Like his *Ellington At Newport 1956 Complete* re-construction, Schaap's research restores rightful integrity to an event which is central to jazz history and listeners from an older time may need to readjust their aural perspectives. But by doing so they will enjoy regular bonuses – an extended "Honeysuckle Rose", including unheard solos from Harry Carney and (remarkably) rhythm guitarist Freddie Green, as well as an extra chorus from trumpeter Buck Clayton and two new band tracks, **Sometimes I'm Happy** and **If Dreams Come True**, as well as the laconic Goodman's one and only in-concert announcement (his later 1950 scripted commentary and tune announcements are also here). Schaap makes a passionate case for CD reproduction of the original 78rpm recordings made on the night, and despite regular crackles, clicks and surface noise he is right; the natural resonance of Carnegie Hall is preserved and central features of Goodman's orchestra – trumpeter James's huge hot-gold sound, Gene Krupa's thundering motivic drums – come over as never before; as, with renewed clarity, does audience applause, both during and after selections and high spots which, of course, include shy Jess Stacy's legendary piano-postscript to the spellbinding **Sing, Sing, Sing** – still jazz's most admirable illustration of getting the last artistic word.

➲ We almost chose **Benny Goodman On The Air 1937–38**, Columbia, 1993

43

Dexter Gordon

Go

Blue Note, 1999 (rec. 1962)

Gordon (tenor-sax), Sonny Clark (piano), Butch Warren (bass), Billy Higgins (drums).

The saga of Dexter Gordon is emblematic of bebop's changing fortunes across the decades, and of the generation of musicians who first played it. Starting in his teens, he was involved in the late swing era, playing with Lionel Hampton, Fletcher Henderson and Louis Armstrong. He was a natural choice when singer Billy Eckstine formed his own big band, which was dominated by players interested in bop. Gordon then became a leading light in small-group bebop and an influence on the young John Coltrane and Sonny Rollins, until sidetracked by addiction and prison sentences in the 1950s.

Re-emerging in the early 1960s and making several fine Blue Note albums, he found the scene generally less than hospitable to his style of music and relocated to Europe for no less than fourteen years. While there, Dexter recorded for various labels and did a superior live series for Black Lion, but his occasional returns to the US were greeted with widespread indifference. In late 1976, however, he was the object of renewed interest and, along with fellow standard-bearers Art Blakey and Betty Carter, started the bebop revival. Rather than a retrospective stance adopted by young musicians, this was a case of quality and experience winning new fans, and the fact that Gordon went on to star in the 1986 movie *Round Midnight* was like a final accolade.

What's remarkable is how little Dexter's style changed between, say, 1946 and 1986. From initial idolization of his hero

Lester Young, his tone and melodic style became far more aggressive, yet, at the same time, precisely calibrated for lagging behind the beat. This mixture of the hot and the cool set listeners on their ears, and galvanized rhythm-sections into playing with sufficient swing to make him catch up with them. The fact that the game of cat and mouse was played out in rhythmic terms only enhanced the relatively simple melodic/harmonic values of his improvised lines, frequently underlined by the use of selective quotation from old popular songs or even older public-domain melodies.

By far the majority of Gordon's best albums find him backed just by piano, bass and drums and perhaps one other horn (it's a pity his late 1940s partnership with tenorist Wardell Gray is not better represented on record). The illusion of witnessing a superior but straight-ahead nightclub set is enhanced by the programming of **Go**, with its four standard songs of differing vintage and two jazz originals. Of the latter, Dexter's own **Cheese Cake** opens the account with two comparatively busy but laidback solos, the first referring both to Lester Young and to Johnny Mercer's "Fools Rush In", one of the many quotations not identified in two sets of inlay-notes. On the other hand, **Second Balcony Jump** is a 1940s item recorded by both the Eckstine and Earl Hines bands, which includes more Lester as well as a reference to Rodgers and Hart's **My Heart Stood Still**".

The sterling work of Billy Higgins on the latter track's closing breaks (done by Art Blakey on the Eckstine version) is a reminder of his marvellously alive playing throughout. Likewise pianist Sonny Clark, who never achieved the reputation that he deserved, solos at the top of his form and accompanies with great alertness, as does Butch Warren. After another, almost-as-good album (*A Swingin' Affair*) had been recorded by the same quartet, Gordon departed for what turned out to be his extended sojourn in Europe, little knowing he was doing research for his role in *Round Midnight*.

⊃We almost chose **Both Sides Of Midnight**, Black Lion, 1988 [1967]

44

Scott Hamilton

Scott Hamilton And Warren Vaché With Scott's Band In New York City

Concord (rec. 1978)

Hamilton (tenor-sax), Warren Vaché (cornet, flugelhorn), Norman Simmons (piano), Chris Flory (guitar), Phil Flanigan (bass), Chuck Riggs (drums), Sue Melikian (vocals).

Now that an A-class generation of New Age American Revivalists – Dan Barrett, Randy Sandke, Harry Allen, Scott Robinson, Ken Peplowski, Howard Alden and their peers – have assured a viable artistic future for pre-modern jazz, it's hard to remember that, by the mid-1970s, that area of the music looked like disappearing for good. In the post-Coltrane world, older values were principally upheld by a waning generation of giants with no one to replace them. Until, that is, the unobtrusive announcement of the arrival in New York of two late-impressionists – tenorist Scott Hamilton and cornettist Warren Vaché junior playing swing music, and proud of it.

Hamilton – at this point still only in his early twenties – both eschewed the currently omnipotent influences of Coltrane and Michael Brecker and re-announced the classic values of Hawkins, Lester Young, Chu Berry and their golden-age contemporaries with elegantly calm confidence and musical heat. His cornet playing partner Vaché (a pupil of trumpeter Pee Wee Erwin) similarly celebrated older heroes from Bunny Berigan to Ruby Braff; his fluid technique, chic vibrato and massive melodic sense combining with creative bravery, which made every one of his solos a triumphant adventure. Their appearance on the international jazz scene – then dominated by jazz fusion and experimentation – prompted universal sighs of relief from a still-heavily populated area of jazz followers who were convinced that soon there would be nothing left to hear.

A quarter of a century on, with the final demise of almost all of their first-generation inspirations, Vaché and Hamilton have risen to the position of father figures to New Wave revivalism. Hamilton has recorded repeatedly in every context from trios to full string orchestras and always flawlessly; Vaché's cornet is that rare thing – a truly personal creative voice whose fluency, architectural sense of melody and unique ability to play sweet, soft and high on his cornet recalls a jazz Heifetz. And, although both these courageous, tenacious and superbly skilled performers now pursue solo careers, their regular partnership, which spanned well over ten years, is one of the triumphs as well as historic high spots of twentieth-century American jazz.

The **New York City** album is a good representative example of their earlier work flanked by a rhythm-section which, apart from Simmons (b. 1929) consisted of equally young (and now equally senior!) contemporaries who had unobtrusively espoused the musical philosophies of their leaders, despite growing up among the rock generation. From Hamilton's breathy sensual opening bars on **Tea For Two**, however, it's obvious that this is no empty repertory but a joyfully committed reaffirmation of jazz values far too important to throw away in the first place. In solo, Vaché's rhythmic flexibility places him somewhere between swing and bebop, but his suave lyrical lines come from a genuinely original concept, and his fearless chance-taking is equalled only by Bunny Berigan in jazz history. The duo's theme-statement on Hamilton's original **Freego** sounds like Coleman Hawkins and Roy Eldridge at their best (Flory has a fine outing here, too) and the final ensemble is as hot as anything ever heard on 52nd street in the 1940s. Vaché's solo on **Darn That Dream** – in turn husky, then openly gold in tone with pealing ascents to the upper register – is championship cornet playing, but Hamilton (his date!) has the last word with a tender **Danny Boy**. With albums like these, everything old was truly new again.

➲No alternative **– this is the only Hamilton/Vaché album currently available**

45

Lionel Hampton

All Star Sessions, Chicago, Hollywood And New York, Volume 2: Hot Mallets

Avid, 1997 (rec. 1937–40)

Hampton (vibraphone, piano, drums, vocals), with groups including Harry James, Ziggy Elman, Irving Randolph (trumpet), Johnny Hodges, Benny Carter, Russell Procope, Chu Berry, Earl Bostic, Jerry Jerome (reeds), Clyde Hart (piano), Allen Reuss, Charlie Christian (guitar), Milt Hinton (bass), Cozy Cole, Sid Catlett, Jo Jones (drums), and others.

Alongside Benny Carter, Lionel Hampton is the last direct link to twentieth-century American jazz's front line talents. The first vibraphonist in jazz – he took up the instrument while working with Les Hite's band – he first recorded on it with Louis Armstrong in 1930 and came to full prominence with Benny Goodman's quartet from November 1936. From that point, Hampton's career was fired by his unflagging energy combined with inspiration and a natural ability to move forward with changing jazz fashion. His big band, first formed in 1941, regularly presented (in records like his classic 1942 "Flying Home") the kind of unleashed elemental excitement which pre-echoed both Norman Granz's wild JATP concerts and subsequently rock'n'roll. And despite an apparent period of artistic semi-consolidation from the 1970s, he was happily, and successfully, recording with rock icons Chaka Khan and Stevie Wonder on the album *For the Sake Of Music* in 1995.

Not unlike Benny Carter, Hampton's significant discography – spanning more than sixty years – presents so much excellence that it demands detailed listening. Some may prefer his definitive teamings with Goodman, his immortal small group *Just Jazz* concert for Gene Norman at Pasadena in 1947 (including an incomparable

"Stardust"), or the 1950s musical meetings with fellow giants like Art Tatum, Oscar Peterson, Stan Getz and Harry Edison or compadres like Mezz Mezzrow. But very hard to forget are Hampton's small-group recordings of the 1930s on which, from 1938, he recorded almost one hundred sides in Chicago, Hollywood and New York. These delicious personifications of small-group swing are sometimes overlooked in the face of stiff contemporary opposition – the glory of Hampton's own work with Goodman, the justifiably immortalized sides that Billie Holiday recorded at the same period with Teddy Wilson, and Wilson's own small-group sessions of the period.

Listening back, it's arguable that Hampton's sides are the best of all. He parades quadruple talents, principally as vibraphonist, but also as premier standard drummer (he played drums with, amongst others, Paul Howard, Louis Armstrong, Eddie Condon and his own big band later), high-speed two-finger pianist, and vocalist. Hampton's ingratiating singing is heard here on a catchy **The Sun Will Shine Tonight**, a tender **I Can Give You Love** and a good-humoured **Stand By For Further Announcements**, and the premier swing stars around him – including Harry James, Benny Carter, Ziggy Elman, Lawrence Brown and many more – are almost invariably sensational. Cootie Williams (a hero wherever he appears here) has an entry, for one, on **Ring Dem Bells**, which (as Humphrey Lyttelton describes it) resembles an express train accelerating from a tunnel! Other standouts include the unstoppable James, urbane Carter and tenorist Chu Berry, whose crying tenor-saxophone sound inimitably partners Hampton on two classic 1939 titles **Sweethearts On Parade** and **Shufflin' At The Hollywood**, as well as two of Hampton's best piano features, the industrious mid-tempo **Denison Swing** and (more typical) high-speed **Wizzin' The Wizz**. A further bonus is the high-level organization of several of these dates; at least sixteen of the sides recorded between July 1938 and October 1939 are perfect microcosms of choreographed prewar swing. Volume 1 of this series, *Open House*, has comparable delights, plus one or two likable oddities, but we mustn't be greedy.

➲We almost chose **All Star Sessions, Volume 1**, Avid, 1997 [1937–41]

46

Herbie Hancock

Head Hunters

Columbia, 1997 (rec.1973)

Hancock (keyboard, synth), Bennie Maupin (reeds, alto flute), Paul Jackson (electric-bass), Harvey Mason (drums), Bill Summers (percussion).

Fusion has received a great deal of bad press, much of it richly deserved. A few of the genre's infamous progeny can usefully be listed here: mindless pyrotechnics, guitar heroics, bland overproduction, strap-on synthesizers and a wholesale lack of swing are only some of the downsides. But the last decade has seen a useful reconsideration of the pros and cons of electric jazz and its original exponents, and fusion's footprints are cropping up in lots of unusual places.

Herbie Hancock was a member of Miles Davis's legendary 1960s quintet, and he made a batch of excellent acoustic records for Blue Note (collected on the six-CD set *Complete Blue Note '60s Sessions*). Early in the 1970s, Hancock began to use electronics and more extensive open improvising in his music, resulting, among others, in the outstanding LP *Sextant*. At this period, in keeping with the black consciousness movement, he adopted the Swahili name "Mwandishi" and gave similar names to the members of his band – Eddie Henderson, Julian Priester, Buster Williams, Billy Hart, and Bennie Maupin, the only musician retained when he revamped the group in 1973 – yet this aspect was set aside, along with the more experimental side of the music. But it was with **Head Hunters**, which became the highest-selling record in the history of jazz shortly after it was released, that Hancock succeeded in breaking through to a mainstream crossover audience the way Miles had wanted to with his electric bands.

Head Hunters was inspired by Davis, but it was a more pop-inflected outing than the trumpeter's comparatively shaggy explorations, and the first track, **Chameleon** – in a version edited down from the nearly sixteen-minute track on the album – was a smash hit, catapulting Hancock into a realm of mass popularity not known in jazz for more than a decade. In hindsight, "Chameleon" is also a terrific, durable piece of music, an insightful merger of 1970s street sounds and new jazz. As layered as filo dough, with carefully orchestrated production and a punchy drum recording, the basic sound takes some of its cues from Jamaican dub, where experimentation and pop go effortlessly together. On the extended take, Bennie Maupin's chiselled tenor sax and Hancock's oozing keyboard are grafted into a sonic cyborg; Hancock takes a highly outré synthesizer solo, culled right from the Sun Ra sourcebook. Meanwhile, slight changes in the mix give an edgy late-psychedelic flavour to bassist Paul Jackson and drummer Harvey Mason's hardcore soul groove.

One thing this record makes clear is that the best of fusion is not, as often misreported, a jazz-rock phenomenon, but is instead a jazz-funk thing. On the deeply funky **Sly** – named after funkmaster Sly Stone, a central influence on Miles's electric music – a slinky opening spills into a bubbling cauldron of modal funk, with an extensive, expressionist soprano-sax solo and the leader's trademark post-Tyner chords on Rhodes electric piano. Hancock pecks out a Meters-ish chicken-scratch rhythm on **Watermelon Man**, updating his 1962 soul-jazz jukebox hit (whose follow-up "Canteloupe Island" was the source of a pop sample for the group US3 in 1997). **Vein Melter** is the disc's slow jam. Maupin's bass-clarinet is bathed in Hancock's synth washes, Bill Summers providing running commentary with percussion details. Slick as hell, but gritty and grimy too, *Head Hunters* is a record that put acid- and lite-jazz on the map. It also puts most of that dribble to shame.

⟳We almost chose **Sextant**, Columbia, 1998 [1972]

Coleman Hawkins

The Ultimate Coleman Hawkins Selected By Sonny Rollins

Verve, 1998 (rec. 1944–57)

Hawkins (tenor-sax), with various groups including Roy Eldridge, Joe Thomas, Buck Clayton (trumpet), Trummy Young (trombone), Ben Webster (tenor sax), Teddy Wilson, Oscar Peterson (piano), Slam Stewart, Israel Crosby, John Kirby, Ray Brown (bass), Cozy Cole, Denzil Best, Sid Catlett (drums), and others.

"Don't you know he was the king of saxophones; yes indeed he was", sings the great Eddie Jefferson on his vocalese transcription of Coleman Hawkins' 1939 classic "Body And Soul". And during jazz music's formative years Hawkins was exactly that – a proud, competitive and kingly musician, who from 1921 on quickly divorced the tenor saxophone from its vaude- ville associations, developed a workable voice for its purposes, and by 1933 – when he recorded for the first time as a leader – had turned his instrument into a powerful medium for jazz expression. Later on, other visionaries – amongst them Lester Young, Bud Freeman and the incomparable Stan Getz – were to retune the tenor saxophone's adaptable voice, but Hawkins was the first, and some would say the most powerful, performer of all.

He was also one of jazz music's natural progressives, who refused to sit back on old victories. After 1943 he was quick to collaborate with the youthful bebop generation, and in 1963 recorded just as easily with post-bop tenorist Sonny Rollins (the compiler of this collection). "I didn't get a competitive feeling when I played with him though", says Rollins. "To me he was just self-assured." By that time Hawkins had already fought his gladiatorial battles, seeking out local opposition in his formative years to best them in cutting competitions. There are occasional on-record reminders of Hawkins' proud supremacy too. At the close of "Crazy Rhythm" from 1937, with his All Star Jam Band (co-featuring Benny Carter and Django Reinhardt), he has the last word with one extra chorus, and photographs of the period show an immaculately dressed hero – a walking proclamation of earned artistic authority.

Rollins' choices for this Verve collection are admirably wide-ranging, beginning with **Picasso**, an unaccompanied tenor-exploration from 1948 which has become known as a definitive demonstration of Hawkins' enveloping tone, fast passionate vibrato and formidable technique. The remainder of the set is principally drawn from his definitive catalogue of 1944 recordings for Keynote, when he was at the height of his powers. Three of these team him with an equally competitive colleague of many years, Roy Eldridge, as well as the elegant giant Teddy Wilson, and the mood is electric in intent; Hawkins' solo entry on **Bean At The Met** is a glove-down challenge and his rhapsodic outing on **I'm In The Mood For Love** seems to challenge the asperity of Eldridge, who nevertheless comes back angrier than ever at the end. Wilson is similarly immaculate on five definitive quartet sides, including **Cattin' At Keynote** and **Just One Of Those Things**, as (on one more) is Buck Clayton, whose cup-mute trumpet is almost submerged beneath Hawkins' huge sound at the conclusion – appropriately perhaps! – of **Under A Blanket Of Blue**.

Regularly throughout these sides, the power of the tenorist seems almost like an elemental cry of victory. Rollins has wisely broadened the span of his collection, however, with the inclusion of tracks from essential 1957 albums on which Hawkins plays **Like Someone In Love** as a feature, then interweaves ravishingly with Ben Webster on the latinate **La Rosita**. Rather surprisingly, Hawkins' original "Body And Soul" is not included, but it appears regularly on other Hawkins compilations, including the one below. Perhaps amid so much great – and less well-known – music the highly qualified compiler of this CD decided there just wasn't room.

⮑We almost chose **Coleman Hawkins 1929–49: Picasso**,

Giants of Jazz, 1992

48

Joe Henderson

Lush Life

Verve, 1992 (rec. 1991)

Henderson (tenor-sax), Wynton Marsalis (trumpet), Stephen Scott (piano), Christian McBride (bass), Gregory Hutchinson (drums).

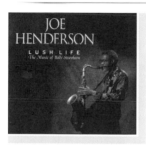

Since he began recording for the Blue Note label, Joe Henderson has ranked among the very top tenor saxophonists. Being closer to Sonny Rollins stylistically than to John Coltrane, whose influence was all-pervasive in the 1960s, probably helped in the long run. He slotted into contexts that took in either fusion or free jazz, while continuing to expand his contribution to the post-bop idiom that brought him to the front in the first place.

Revered by hardcore musicians and fans he may have been, but beyond that his name meant little. Then, in his mid-fifties, he was signed by a big label. They suggested a concept to him – an album devoted to the compositions of Duke Ellington's collaborator, Billy Strayhorn – and put him alongside four upcoming tyros. The outcome could truly be called a hit with the public. **Lush Life**, the album, topped the *Billboard* jazz charts for several weeks in 1992 and Henderson's unaccompanied version of the title tune won a Grammy award.

The twist in the tale, as the last sentence implies, is he did it without synthesizers, bass guitars, strings or a choir. This is straight jazz, from the full quintet that plays on three tracks right down to the various permutations that include the familiar **Take The A Train** as a belligerently successful duet between tenor sax and drummer Gregory Hutchinson.

Moreover, the concept justified itself by bringing to the forefront the sound Henderson produces from the higher register. A fluted sound with the barest wisp of breathiness that fleetingly makes one think of the soprano, it had not stood out in the way Stan Getz's ravishing top notes became a trademark because Henderson did not get involved regularly with the kind of material that invited it.

That sound, indeed, hits you from the first notes of the opening track. Though **Isfahan** seems a straightforward duet between Henderson and bass prodigy Christian McBride, the arrangement is significantly credited to Don Sickler, who no doubt came up with the gambit. There's more of that kind of beauty on **Blood Count**; Henderson's reading may be reflective compared to what Getz, let alone Johnny Hodges, did with it, but no less moving. Of the other ballads, **Lotus Blossom**, a duet with Stephen Scott, emerges as a triumph for the pianist, who conjures up a crafty introduction and gets the opening solo, to which he imparts a touch of stride. Aged 22 when he cut the album, Scott has yet to break through as a leader, but recent work in Sonny Rollins's group indicates his enormous talent.

The quintet appears on Sickler's arrangement of **A Flower Is A Lovesome Thing**. Trumpet and saxophone split the first chorus and each take a solo, Henderson's velvety sound and the way his ideas balance each other producing a classic that Wynton Marsalis matches through his own glistening tone and by making the difficult easy. On the more attacking **Johnny Come Lately**, Marsalis reminds one a trifle of Clark Terry, and everyone enjoys the juicy chord sequence of **U.M.M.G.**

Drawing Room Blues by a tenor piano bass trio is superb. As for **Lush Life** itself, not the easiest tune to squeeze something from at the best of times – let alone when completely unsupported – Henderson keeps his poise, leads effortlessly from verse to main theme, lets the notes ring and ends on yet another high.

➲We almost chose **Inner Urge**, Blue Note, 1989 [1964]

49

Woody Herman

This Is Jazz

Columbia, 1995 (rec. 1945–65).

Herman (clarinet, alto sax), with groups including Pete Candoli, Neil Hefti, Bill Chase (trumpet), Bill Harris (trombone), Flip Phillips, Stan Getz, Zoot Sims, Serge Chaloff, Sal Nistico (reeds), Ralph Burns, Nat Pierce (piano), Marjorie Hyams (vibraphone), Dave Tough, Jake Hanna (drums) et al.

Some jazz artists don't receive their just deserts in terms of CD reissue, and one of them is certainly Woody Herman. Despite a proliferating programme, there has yet to materialize a compilation as comprehensive as the three-volume *Thundering Herds*, produced by Frank Driggs for CBS between 1959 and 1961. This richly satisfying set has yet to reappear; hopefully it waits in the wings.

While Woody Herman's phenomenal recording career spanned over five decades (1936–87), lovers of his music home in on three periods and orchestras: The Swingin' Herman Herd of the 1960s (featuring trumpeters Bill Chase and Dusko Goykovich, trombonist Henry Southall, tenorist Sal Nistico, pianist Nat Pierce and drummer Jake Hanna); the New Third Herd of 1952–53 (which recorded the well-remembered "Blues In Advance" and, most memorably of all, the First and Second Herds.

Herman's First Herd, which he assembled in 1944, was a completely new project, aptly described by his biographer Gene Lees as "the most advanced, innovative and adventurous of its time". Staffed by brilliant arrangers – including Ralph Burns, Eddie Sauter and Dave Matthews – and loaded with new stars (trumpeter "Superman" Pete Candoli, anarchic trombonist Bill Harris, tenorist Flip Phillips and a rhythm-section featuring vibraphonist Marjorie

Hyams and powered by bassist Chubby Jackson and drummer Dave Tough), the band's first recording was a head arrangement, "Apple Honey", quickly followed by "I Wonder", "Laura", and one of Herman's most enduring hits, **Caldonia**, with its unison five-trumpet extravaganza scored by Neil Hefti. Other Herman's triumphs at this point included **Northwest Passage**, "Wild Root", trombonist Harris' classic **Bijou**, the lunatic "Your Father's Moustache" and three movements of Ralph Burns' **Summer Sequence**, along with Herman's signature tune, **Woodchopper's Ball**.

In common with Benny Goodman, Tommy Dorsey, Harry James and Jack Teagarden, Herman broke up his band in 1946 but in autumn 1947 returned with his Second Herd including (to begin with) a five-man saxophone team led by altoist Sam Marowitz and completed by the "Four Brothers" – Stan Getz, Zoot Sims, Herbie Steward (replaced by Al Cohn) and Serge Chaloff. This orchestra (which recorded hastily in December 1947 for Columbia, prior to a second recording ban by James Petrillo) similarly produced classics including **Keen And Peachy**, **The Goof And I**, **Four Brothers** and **Summer Sequence Part Four**, featuring a Stan Getz solo which would instantly establish him as a luminous solo talent. Herman's Second Herd was even better than his first, but despite a re-signing to Capitol (and subsequent re-recording of part four of "Summer Sequence" – now retitled "Early Autumn", with ever-more exquisite Getz, plus a new hit, "Lemon Drop" – it disbanded in 1949.

Included from Herman's First Herd in this collection are "Northwest Passage", "Caldonia", "Bijou", **Everywhere**, **Sidewalks Of Cuba**, "Woodchopper's Ball" and **Happiness Is Just A Thing Called Joe**, with vocals by Francis Wayne. From the Second Herd comes "Summer Sequence Part Four", "Keen And Peachy", **I've Got News For You** and "The Goof And I", plus 1960s tracks from Herman's Swingin' Herd, including Bill Chase's **23 Red**, **Greasy Sack Blues** and a live "Northwest Passage". A good start for a great bandleader that no respectable jazz book may omit.

⮌We almost chose **Woody Herman At Carnegie Hall 1946**, Verve, 1999

50

Earl Hines

Live At The New School/I've Got The World On A String

Chiaroscuro, 1988 (rec. 1973)

Hines (solo piano).

"There will probably be less than twenty or so musicians that will be considered the giants of this type of music we now call jazz", writes producer Hank O'Neal on the sleeve of this album, "and Earl Hines will be one of the chosen few, and every note will be important!" In a book as selective as this, such statements are worthy of supportive evidence, but there can be very few who would question O'Neal's claim to begin with.

With his "trumpet-style" piano in the 1920s, Hines was the first soloist to audibly challenge the new supremacy of Louis Armstrong – a daring invasion which kept the two men at arm's length for much of their lives ("Too many All Stars", Armstrong observed ruefully, if indirectly, of the pianist's tenure in his group later on, "make bad friends!"). Nonetheless, Hines' influence in the formative years of jazz was colossal; his polyrhythmic virtuosity, chiming chordal conceptions and vivid pearl-bright single lines scattered with almost ostentatious ease, influenced everyone from the subsequently unconquerable Art Tatum to more discreet, yet no less precious, talents like Jess Stacy. Hines survived the decades that followed with a big band, with Armstrong again (from 1948 to 1951) and later on the West Coast at the Hangover Club in San Francisco for five years, leading his own Dixieland sextet. These were steady rather than remarkable times, but in 1964 he triumphantly, if unexpectedly, re-established himself with two sensational concerts at New York's Little Theatre. These were programmed by Stanley Dance (who thereafter arranged new recording dates for Hines) and a long piece about the veteran pianist, by Whitney Balliett, appeared in the *New Yorker*. "It really changed the whole course of my career and opened doors for me," Hines remembered later, "and from then on I had a new spirit!". For the last twenty years of his life, accordingly, he triumphantly re-established himself as a celebrity, toured Russia, Japan, Italy and Europe; played for President Ford at the White House in 1976 and was voted top pianist in *Downbeat*'s International Critic's Poll for seven years.

Hines' discography from this period is rich with treasures and many of them are solo recordings. Like Art Tatum, his exuberance and super-creativity (as well as sense of celebrity) regularly led him irresistibly to musical centre stage and, like Louis Armstrong, he had endless set pieces with which to raise roofs. One of them at least – **Boogie Woogie On St. Louis Blues**, with a ringing right-hand ostinato retained for chorus after chorus before the piece finishes – is on this album too, which, from its opening track, reveals Hines at the height of his renaissance. Lightning runs from top to bottom of the keyboard, trumpet-like shakes at the end of right-hand chords (a device directly borrowed by Jess Stacy), daring polyrhythms, ever-shifting harmonies, and dramatically conflicting left- and right-hand single-line patterns are all part of the Hines style that makes pianistic monuments of lone ballads like **It's The Talk Of The Town**, extended medleys including one for Fats Waller (concluding with "Honeysuckle Rose') and another bravura exploration of Bernstein's *West Side Story*, as well as the album's greatest track – a magnificent transformation of **I've Got The World On A String**, which constantly surprises, notably with a symphonic counter-theme towards the end. Hines' announcements are retained and aficionados will delight in the cover art – a wonderfully witty oil-impression of the pianist by lyricist and lifelong man-about-jazz, John DeVries. Great deal, O'Neal!

⮑We almost chose **Jazz In Paris: Paris One Night Stand**, Gitanes, 2001 [1957]

51

Billie Holiday

Lady Day's 25 Greatest 1933–44

ASV Living Era, 1996 (rec. 1933–44)

Billie Holiday (vocals), with Benny Goodman and his Orchestra, Teddy Wilson and his Orchestra, Count Basie and his Orchestra, Billie Holiday's Orchestra, The Esquire All-Star Jam Band, Eddie Heywood Sextet, Toots Camarata Orchestra.

The recording career of Billie Holiday may reveal a more dramatic span of emotional change than any other jazz artist. Recently it has been widely argued that her later work, while often more painful, is correspondingly more profound; trumpeter Buck Clayton – a pivotal figure in Billie's prewar recorded masterpieces – averred that, late on in life, "Billie continued to improve with time until the time that she expired." Other listeners may revert back irresistibly to the early Holiday years, when – given the right material, surroundings and day – she could enchant you with a youthful meld of open-hearted vocal joy, spiced with graduate sensuality. The abundance of winning swing songs blossoming on the musical landscape by the mid-1930s helped the illusion, of course. But even close to the start of her career (for example, on "I Wished On The Moon", from 1935), there is already the audible hint of later weight on her shoulders and it would be an over-simplification to claim that Holiday was happy on record until 1940 and mournful thereafter.

Lady Day's 25 Greatest (once again compiled by the infallible Vic Bellerby) is therefore right to resist the implication, and certainly does so. It offers a balanced eleven-year span of Holiday's earlier career beginning with one of her two first recorded titles (**Your Mother's Son-in-law** from 1933, with Benny Goodman) and ending in 1944 with a pair of titles produced by Milt Gabler and recorded for Decca with Toots Camarata's orchestra. These considerably include the superior ballad **That Ole Devil Called Love** by Allan Roberts and Doris Fisher, which (along with the neglected **You Better Go Now**) is one of her most enchanting orchestral recordings of the period, and which – via British singer Alison Moyet – helped to revive interest in Billie Holiday in Britain in the mid-1980s. In between are numerous Holiday standards, which (as regularly in Bellerby's selections) combine musical celebrity and content. Amongst them are classics with Teddy Wilson's orchestra, including **Miss Brown To You**, the headlong **What A Little Moonlight Can Do**, **Moanin' Low** (with Hodges's sensual alto and Cootie Williams' murmuring growl-trumpet commentary) and four near-incomparable cuts combining the kingly triumvirate of Lester Young, Clayton and Wilson with Billie: **I Must Have That Man**, **Easy Living**, **I'll Never Be The Same** and a sublime **Back In Your Own Back Yard**. These tracks, involving her favourite tenorist and Clayton ("prettiest man I ever saw!") sound like musical lovemaking, and Bellerby has also cherry-picked the sublime **Did I Remember** from 1936 (with Bunny Berigan, Artie Shaw and Joe Bushkin). Four live recordings with Count Basie (1937) and the Esquire All-Star Jam Band (1944) are valuable as, at this time, Holiday was almost invariably recorded in studio, and four more, from 1939, by her orchestra include (untypically) a pair of blues (the Ellingtonian **Long Gone Blues** with Tab Smith's climbing soprano-saxophone plus Hot Lips Page's speaking trumpet, and **Fine And Mellow**), plus **Some Other Spring** and a slightly over-jolly **Them There Eyes**. On these tracks the ghost of Holiday's later melancholia is already whispering in the mists, and once named in the next mournful minor key (**Ghost Of Yesterday**, with formidable lyrics by Arthur Herzog) it appears in full view on track 25 – the horrifying **Strange Fruit** (a protest song about black lynchings) which changed Holiday instantly into the controversial tragedienne she would unwittingly remain for life. A fine – if occasionally leisurely paced – recorded introduction to jazz's most luckless diva.

⟲ No alternative – **nothing else as comprehensive**

52

Abdullah Ibrahim

African River

Enja, 1989

Ibrahim (piano), Howard Johnson (trumpet, tuba, baritone-sax), Robin Eubanks (trombone), Horace Alexander Young (soprano-sax, alto-sax, piccolo), John Stubblefield (tenor-sax, flute), Buster Williams (bass), Brian Adams (drums).

Then known as Dollar Brand, Abdullah Ibrahim was the first jazz musician of genuine stature from South Africa to emigrate during the apartheid regime. Duke Ellington encouraged him to head from Europe to New York, where he developed further an approach to music that blends African rhythms and melodies with American-style jazz improvisation.

As Ellington and another inspiration, Thelonious Monk, did, he brought to the jazz ensemble a fresh sensibility. But compared (in particular) to Monk he can be self-effacing as pianist-leader. His solo style often displays complex left-hand patterns that make the most impact when heard alone. Furthermore, he does not always write himself quite so prominently into the arrangements, though **Chisa**, an exuberant township theme whose rhythm resembles that of a calypso, offers a significant exception as piano figures nudge against Horace Alexander Young's saxophone lead. On the longest tracks, **African River** itself and **Duke 88**, Ibrahim doesn't even take a solo.

Ekaya, an African word for "home", was the name given to the larger American-based groups he led from about the mid-1980s. One of the later versions appears on **African River** in a typical line-up of trombone and three saxophones, though Howard Johnson adds a dimension by switching occasionally to tuba and, on **Sweet Samba**, taking a trumpet solo. The opening **Toi Toi**, another with interlocking kwela-type rhythms, is dominated by Young's soprano from which he produces a harsh, wailing sound, closer to Bechet than to any contemporary. He takes a similar outgoing role on "Chisa".

A fairly abstract preamble to "African River" eases into the theme that unwinds from a mellifluous passage of piano against ensemble chords. Ibrahim invariably writes strong melodies and designs the riffs or backgrounds needed to cushion solos. The soloists get stuck in over the clip-clopping Latin beat, as they do on "Sweet Samba", though that closes with its typical blast from John Stubblefield's tenor on the final bridge. Ibrahim does not feature himself on either number and also restricts his role on **Joan – Capetown Flower**, a ballad expressed through the glowingly warm tones drawn from the horns. This track is one to which Buster Williams, among the best bassists around, makes a crucial contribution.

The feeling evoked of pastoral solemnity, lightly coated with the bite of his township pieces, and the way he interprets such songs, perhaps represents the overriding image conveyed by Ibrahim's music. He realizes this to perfection on "Duke 88", the spacious melody with inbuilt breaks leading to a round of solos backed by sonorous chords. A relaxed Robin Eubanks opens, his sound gruff and warm; Johnson makes the handover seamless, ending at the top of the baritone's range; Stubblefield, who leads the line brilliantly, caps a smooth entry with fireworks during the stop-time passage, fervently mixing Jackie McLean and Arthur Blythe, and Young on alto completes the round.

Two classic Ibrahim themes close the album, and on these his piano takes wing. After brief introductions to **The Wedding** and **The Mountain Of The Night**, he continually underpins the ensemble. The first is led by Young in typically extrovert style (Ibrahim needs musicians not afraid to let emotions hang out). On the second, flute and piccolo carry the tune over a beat that ripples gently underneath to give the ballad form a tinge of township lilt.

⮑We almost chose **African Piano**, ECM, undated [1969]

53

Harry James

Yes, Indeed!

ASV Living Era, 1993 (rec. 1936–42)

James (trumpet, vocals), with The Dean and his Kids, Benny Goodman and his Orchestra, Teddy Wilson's Quartet, Lionel Hampton and his Orchestra, The Boogie Woogie Trio, Harry James Orchestra.

After Louis Armstrong, Harry James was the most powerful and spectacular trumpeter of his generation. While lacking Armstrong's majesty of conception, his legendary technique and nerveless command – married to audacious musical imagination – turned him into the premier trumpet voice of the Swing era as well as a star beyond the jazz galaxy. Slim, handsome and a lady's man, James first attracted universal attention with Benny Goodman's orchestra, regularly playing lead trumpet and delivering solos notable for their massive tone, strength and energy. "He ripped at a solo", Irving Townsend famously wrote "as if he hadn't had one in weeks!" By 1939 he was leading his own band, as he would continue to do until his death in July 1983.

James was a remarkably gifted man, as well as a multilevelled personality. But his trumpeter's fondness for sweet ballads, sexily played (such as **You Made Me Love You**, his first mega-hit from 1941), as well as Hollywood popularity (he appeared in numerous films and married Betty Grable in 1943) regularly led postwar jazz critics to dub James "commercial", or to lionize lesser talents, however capable, such as the now-legendary Bunny Berigan, who, unlike his resilient contemporary, died early of drink. James nevertheless seemed impervious to such minor-league criticisms – his talents had turned him into a teenage idol early on, and later attempts to rewrite the jazz credo meant little to him. After a brief period of retirement, his career recharged in the mid-1950s with a new band featuring arrangements by Neil Hefti, Ernie Wilkins and Thad Jones, and it was a pity that Count Basie's use of an identical team of arrangers (notably Hefti in 1957 on *The Complete Atomic Basie*) sometimes left James' band neglected. Nevertheless, his passionate, often blues-imbued trumpet remained one of jazz's most elemental sounds for another twenty years; his technical mastery meant that the adoption of more contemporary trumpet vocabulary was a simple matter if required, and even today listening back to his records illustrates that very few more powerful trumpeters, if any, have ever been heard within the jazz spectrum.

ASV's **Yes, Indeed!** collection covers James' work from 1936 to 1942, as usual combining fame with overall musical representation (and excellence) in their selections. These follow James' career in chronological pattern, picking up at two sides with Ben Pollack from 1936 – the headlong **Spreadin' Rhythm Around** (where Townsend's encomium is perfectly illustrated by James' ferocious entry and chorus, a benchmark for jazz trumpet) and **Zoom Zoom Zoom**, with his ingratiating vocal to the fore. Then come two tracks illustrating the fire he lent to Benny Goodman (red-hot on **Wrappin' It Up**) before a pair of important small-group sides – **Jubilee** and **Life Goes To A Party** – which James recorded during this period using a mixed band including Count Basie cornermen. Other important small-group cuts include three essential inclusions – the classic **Boo Woo** and **Woo Woo**, with Pete Johnson's Boogie Woogie Trio and **Just A Mood** with Teddy Wilson and xylophonist Red Norvo, which has some of the finest and most poised jazz trumpet blues on record. Then we are on to eleven tracks by James' big band from 1939 to 1942 including one song each by three of his best singers – Frank Sinatra, Dick Haymes and Helen Forrest – and three indelible James classics including "You Made Me Love You", **Two-O'-Clock Jump** and **Ciribiribin**, all of which stayed in the repertoire of this powerful charismatic super-talent for life. A well-judged compendium.

⮑We almost chose **Harry James & His Orchestra**, Giants of Jazz, 1994 [1954–66]

54

Keith Jarrett

The Köln Concert

ECM, undated (rec. 1975)

Jarrett (piano).

Keith Jarrett is one of the most prodigiously talented and most prolifically documented musicians of the last thirty years. As a result, he's been highly influential and it's rare to find a pianist under 40 who isn't using his language or at least heavily marked by it. On the other hand, Jarrett is actively reviled by some for his opinions and his posturing, both intellectual and physical. It's also possible for the listener to take up a third position – as when discussing Jelly Roll Morton, for instance – of disliking his personality but admiring his music.

He has been a dynamic performer ever since the late 1960s quartet of saxophonist Charles Lloyd (which he helped gain its popular following by joining at the age of 21, when his gyrating mannerisms and his vocal exclamations were already in place). A fruitful period with Miles Davis, including a European tour, led to his first unaccompanied album for ECM (*Facing You*), after which he turned his back forever on electric keyboards to concentrate on the traditional piano. He ran two simultaneous quartets in the 1970s a much-recorded New York-based one with saxophonist Dewey Redman (e.g. *Expectations*, Columbia) and a Scandinavian group with Jan Garbarek (*My Song*, ECM). He also found time to concertize as a soloist, the activity for which he's best known to the widest number of listeners.

The Köln Concert is the one that has now sold in excess of two million units. A late 1960s/early 1970s trend had already shown that piano solo albums were relatively simple (read:

inexpensive) to produce and that they reached a wider audience who didn't like all those horns and drums – such exposure benefited performers as complex as Earl Hines and Cecil Taylor. But, in Jarrett's case, the music also appealed to a constituency accustomed to attending recitals of European nineteenth- and twentieth-century piano works, and the pianist's wide knowledge of that repertoire blended with his improvisatory expertise to bring a taste of jazz to a whole new clientele.

The most celebrated section of the concert, titled **Part I**, clearly demonstrates Jarrett's approach, which places considerable reliance on repetitious backing figures (ostinatos). The sparse, out-of-tempo introduction in A minor leads to a laidback Latin rhythm with some gospel-piano figurations, the right hand becoming more florid around the 4:00 mark. A simple harmonic turnaround and more insistent rhythm is emphasized at 6:30 by Jarrett's momentary foot-stamping, with a melody recalling Elton John before the improvisation takes off again. The harmonic basis only changes around 13:00, with jazzy passing-chords gradually introducing a more lyrical feel at 14:30. This evolves around 17:30 into a "classical piano" sound with added jazz phrasing, before a repeated harp effect in A major at 20:00 is crowned by a rock rhythm that carries through almost to the conclusion at over 25 minutes.

Other remarkable moments include the minor-key funk at 15:00 into **Part II** (indexed as "Part IIb" only because it began on side three of the vinyl edition) and the encore, **Part IIc**, which recalls "Part I" but without repeating it. This whole unedited performance contained the seeds not only of countless other Jarrett solo concerts but of much other work. Everything – his recordings of European classical repertoire and of his own written compositions, the frankly self-indulgent multi-instrumental overdubbing of *Spirits* and the successful updating of Bill Evans's approach in the many albums by his Standards Trio (with two former Evans sidemen, Gary Peacock and Jack DeJohnette) – is put into perspective by *The Köln Concert*.

⮌We almost chose **Expectations**, Columbia, 1999 [1972]

55

Bunk Johnson

The King Of The Blues

American Music, 1989 (rec. 1944)

Johnson (trumpet), George Lewis (clarinet), Jim Robinson (trombone), Lawrence Marrero (banjo), Alcide "Slow Drag" Pavageau (bass), Baby Dodds (drums), Sidney "Jim Little" Brown (tuba) added for two tracks.

The American jazz revival was only just under way when William Russell founded the American Music label in 1944 and recorded the legendary trumpeter Bunk Johnson with clarinettist George Lewis and trombonist "Big Jim" Robinson – a triumvirate which, in future, would come to personify authentic New Orleans music. Many people consider these beautiful recordings (first issued on 12" 78s and later in the early 1950s on 10" LPs) to rank alongside those of King Oliver and Jelly Roll Morton as the most important of their genre. The sound equipment Russell used is a permanent part of the George H. Buck Jazz Foundation museum display in New Orleans, and it is Buck's exemplary label which has now issued the American Music series in full on CD.

These records are historically comparable to Oliver and Morton, but for different reasons. Johnson and Lewis re-emerged years later in the music's history when its first creative heat had subsided and the Swing era was imposing an unacceptable commercial veneer over a music which had come into being as a vital and vibrant process of joyful self-expression. The recordings of Johnson, Lewis and their contemporaries stripped away the formalization (as well as much of the spectacular technique) which had entered the music from the later 1920s, and set in its place an unadorned statement of purely musical intent which both reiterated fundamentals as to what jazz was about, and questioned the validity of its current preoccupations. It was at this point that considerations of "authenticity" entered the music, creating a new aesthetic that praised musical honesty and shunned device in any form – a deeply valid artistic viewpoint too often mislaid today.

The King Of The Blues contains Johnson's first recordings for American Music, and William Russell's sleevenotes on this first album passionately draw attention to Johnson's immense skills as a blues trumpeter, as well as to the regular praises of his skills by high-profile critics such as Virgil Thompson. In 1943, Thompson wrote: "Bunk is an artist of delicate imagination, meditative in style rather than flashy, and master of the darkest trumpet-tone I have ever heard." Significantly, Thompson also wrote of the music, "Nobody tried to show how fast he could play or how high, nor tried to conceal the tune. Nothing could be less sentimental, or speak more seriously from the heart, or be less jittery. Certainly no music was ever less confused." No better summary of the fine qualities of New Orleans jazz may have been set down.

On this album Johnson plays thirteen blues titles, widely varied in tempo, mood and structure. His relationship with Lewis and Robinson may have been personally uneasy, but the unadorned conviction of their on-record music remains amid the natural echo of the ambience in which the music was recorded. Quite a lot is ensemble-based (as jazz was pre-Armstrong, in general), but clarinettist Lewis and trombonist Robinson both solo superbly on **Dippermouth Blues**, **Midnight Blues** and regularly elsewhere, while Johnson both leads and solos with dignity and flare. The marvellous **Weary Blues** is a definitive example of a great New Orleans jazz band in full flight. When this music was first heard it was sometimes criticized for incidental technical problems of tuning or technical accuracy, but it is important to remember that great jazz – like speech – cannot, and should not, always demonstrate word perfection for fear of falsehood.

⊃ No alternative – **a classic album**

56

Stan Kenton

New Concepts Of Artistry In Rhythm

Capitol, 1989 (rec. 1952)

Kenton (piano), big band including Conte Candoli, Maynard Ferguson (trumpet),
Frank Rosolino, Bill Russo (trombone), Lee Konitz (alto-sax), Richie Kamuca, Bill
Holman (tenor-sax), Stan Levey (drums), Gerry Mulligan (arranger, composer).

All the successful big-band leaders
were PR-conscious, and Kenton
was for a long time more successful
and more conscious than most.
"Artistry In Rhythm" was his
original marketing tag in the mid-
1940s, followed by his late 1940s
"Progressive Jazz" (the term's first
use) and the early 1950s
"Innovations In Modern Music".
Following this costly experiment,
the **New Concepts** era (and much of Stan's later music) represented something of a return to his roots, with a swinging outfit capable of playing for dancers while bursting with loftier ambitions.

The repertoire for the 1952–54 outfit was mainly written by
two sidemen, trombonist Bill Russo and tenorman Bill Holman.
They effected some useful combinations of the leader's previously established signature sounds, such as blaring trumpets and
simultaneously brash-and-mellow trombones, with the lighter,
more rhythmic approach associated with ex-Kenton arranger
Shorty Rogers (and with Gerry Mulligan, who never played for
Kenton but contributes two fine scores here, **Swing House** –
based on "Sweet Georgia Brown" – and **Young Blood**). This
was highly appropriate, since the quota of jazz soloists was
stronger than in some previous editions, with Candoli's boppish
trumpet, Konitz's reserved intellectuality, Kamuca's relaxed swing
and Rosolino's exhilarating trombone backed by a lively rhythm-
section starring former Gillespie drummer Stan Levey.

This expanded reissue begins with a rather unfortunate addition, though one could hardly put a track called **Prologue** anywhere else. Over an episodic, ten-minute composition by Russo designed to spotlight every one of the band's nineteen members, Kenton declaims a monologue about their qualities and his unifying aims – it would be nice to hear it without the overdubbed philosophizing. But the subsequent tracks, retaining the running order of the original album with a further couple of extras from the same sessions, mostly feature the soloists at greater length, and give a more practical demonstration of their abilities and the band's ensemble flair.

The frequently tasteless Maynard Ferguson is used to good effect alongside guitarist Sal Salvador in the humorous counterpoint of Holman's **Invention**, while Russo's contributions include well-crafted spots for Candoli (**Portrait Of A Count**) and Rosolino (**Frank Speaking**). The soloist who gets the most space is the one least expected to accept a salary from Kenton in the first place, Lee Konitz, former acolyte of the ascetic Lennie Tristano. He's heard with other soloists, sometimes creating simultaneously, on the two-part **Improvisation**, and alone on the ballad **My Lady**. Finally, he and Rosolino both have solos on the description of Havana, **23° N–82° W**, something of a Latin-jazz classic.

Kenton's early hit singles, including straight-swing items like "Eager Beaver" and a famous version of the Latin standard "Peanut Vendor", later appeared on compilations such as *The Best Of* or *Jazz Profile: Stan Kenton*. But he was also one of the first bandleaders to exploit the unifying concepts of the LP era, beginning with the elephantine forty-piece "Innovations" orchestra, which brought forth Bob Graettinger's "modern-classical" suite *City Of Glass*, while works by that band's many other contributors are collected on *Innovations In Modern Music*. The era ushered in by the album under review also begat further material (reissued as *Showcase*), and later highlights included *Cuban Fire* and *Adventures In Time*, both written by Johnny Richards. All of these are on Capitol, but *New Concepts* most successfully balances composerly individuality and jazz expertise.

↪ We almost chose **Cuban Fire**, Capitol, 1991 [1956–60]

57

Roland Kirk

Rip, Rig And Panic/Now Please Don't You Cry, Beautiful Edith

Verve, 1990 (rec. 1965 67)

Kirk (reeds, flutes), Jaki Byard, Lonnie Licton Smith (piano), Richard Davis, Ronnie Boykins (bass), Elvin Jones, Grady Tate (drums).

One of the best-known icons of jazz: a burly blind man with wraparound shades, some funky chapeau, neck slung with saxophones, whistles, flutes and noise-makers that dangle like dead birds after a successful hunt. The spectacular image of Roland Kirk (late in the 1960s he prefixed his name with Rahsaan) has always threatened to interfere with his historical significance and the immense swathe of his artistic path. Struck blind in a medical accident when he was two – an event memorialized the title of his stunning 1968 LP *The Inflated Tear* – Kirk grew up to be one of jazz's most flamboyant showboaters, utilizing trick saxophone techniques like slap-tongue, harmonics and circular breathing, wielding unusual and archaic instruments like stritch and manzello, and constituting a one-man sax section by playing multiple horns at the same time, a throwback to novelty players like clarinettist Wilbur Sweatman. But all the effects, all the gimmicks, were put to the highest musical ends.

The summit of Kirk's works is his quartet session **Rip, Rig And Panic**, released on EmArcy in 1965. When Verve packaged it for reissue, they paired it with **Now You Don't Cry, Beautiful Edith**, an eclectic outing from two years later. It's cool as a bonus, with the fun r&b romp **Fallout**, some zany echo effects on **It's A Grand Night For Swinging**, the endless one-note ride through **Blue Rol**, and a relatively rare appearance by stellar Sun Ra bassist Ronnie Boykins. But the real meat of the matter is in the former date, which endures as one of the most rewarding 35 minutes in recorded jazz. The tough opener, **No Tonic Pres**, gives instant evidence of Kirk's tenor greatness. An original composition – written in memory of Lester Young – it sports an ambiguous tonal centre (hence the title) that provides ample springboard for extrapolation. Jaki Byard's sweeping in-and-out piano solo points the way for Don Pullen, and he deftly slips in a bit of stride; he peppers **From Bechet, Byas And Fats** with Walleresque woogie, while the saxophonist plays another huge tenor solo in homage to thick-lined hero Don Byas, returning to the soprano-like manzello in the theme. He also explores some Trane-like manzello (recall, he's using Coltrane's drummer!) on the waltz **Black Diamond**. Kirk punctuates his tender tenor statement on the jaw-dropping ballad **Once In A While** with fat sax chords, and he provides his own singing counter-line as the piece comes to a rolling boil.

Two pieces on the disc are among Kirk's most adventurous. The title track, which he said was inspired by composer Edgard Varèse, starts with an arresting set of sax harmonics, Davis's scrubbing arco and dissonant piano, which climax with a recording of breaking glass, hard-edited into Kirk's sly drumless theme, then careening tenor and aggressive piano solos, with Elvin Jones thundering forward into more nasty harmonics, the theme recap, and a terrifying electronic outro in which Kirk smacks an amp with spring-reverb. The record's closer, **Slippery, Hippery, Flippery**, conjoins walkie-talkie voices and taped sounds to the acoustic quartet (blowing white-hot, it should be mentioned), anticipating some of the dubbish multi-tracking and editing concepts of electric Miles Davis groups by years. He would go on to make even more elaborate use of production, but this raw first appearance of electronics in Kirk's oeuvre comes as an unforgettable jolt.

⊃We almost chose **The Inflated Tear**, Atlantic, 1988 [1968]

58

Lee Konitz

Alone Together

Blue Note, 1997 (rec. 1996)

Konitz (alto-sax), Brad Mehldau (piano), Charlie Haden (bass).

Jointly credited to all three musicians, this album (and a companion set from the same night club sessions, *Another Shade Of Blue*) speaks positively about the health of jazz in the 1990s. A debate has opened up about the so-called conflict between tradition and ... well, if not innovation, then further exploration of recent developments. The conflict would be entirely spurious, were it not for questions of money and subsidized performance, since all the major figures of jazz have paid due attention to both imperatives – either innovating and then reinforcing the tradition or, more often, doing both simultaneously.

At the time of recording, Haden was in his sixtieth year, Mehldau (a late addition to what was planned as a duo) in his mid-twenties and Konitz pushing seventy, with no signs of slowing up. From his early association with the opinionated pianist Lennie Tristano, through his work with what should have been inhospitable big bands (Claude Thornhill and Stan Kenton), Konitz has always ploughed a lonely furrow. He demonstrated his individuality in the late 1940s heyday of bebop by failing to sound anything like Charlie Parker while nevertheless learning from the rhythmic freedom of Bird and of their common hero, Lester Young.

Contributing his unusual alto tone to the Miles Davis *Birth Of The Cool* band, Konitz became a leader of his own ad hoc groups in the 1950s and has never looked back in terms of either formats or colleagues, happily appearing in any setting that allows him to improvise (including completely unaccompanied performances). Yet he remains wedded to the Tristano tenet that, to improvise on a chord sequence with the necessary freedom, it should be one that the soloist knows inside out and, preferably, has played hundreds of times before. As a result, the most recent composition here is Monk's **Round Midnight**, while the other five long discussions involve Tin Pan Alley classics of the 1930s, such as **Cherokee**, **The Song Is You** and the title track. Lee's rhythmic ingenuity and vast melodic repertoire surfaces in the almost subliminal quotations liberally spicing his lines, although perhaps the most unexpected example is Haden's insertion of his "Song For Che" into **What Is This Thing Called Love?**

Haden is clearly a musician who now mines the tradition (with his Quartet West project) rather than being on the cutting edge with Ornette Coleman or his own Liberation Music Orchestra. Yet he was already a traditionalist then – with a swinging four-to-the-bar pulse and an ability to turn corners telepathically – while his playing in the present wide-open space reflects an approach that is anything but hidebound. Sonically balanced so as not to distract from the three-way interplay (Haden co-produced the recording with Konitz), his subtlety and reticence is enhanced by sticking to the bass's lower register. The precocious pianist, meanwhile, plays more sparsely than on his own albums without holding back on harmonic invention, especially when Konitz lays out.

The album has a suitably unfinished feel, with a couple of tracks fading just before they end (probably because they continued uninterrupted into another tune). Whereas much of the music recommended in this book seems "perfect" – both cause and effect of its classic status – the altoist's aim is always to produce something that could only exist at the moment it's played. That he has succeeded for over fifty years, and with collaborators as different as Tristano (*Sub-Conscious Lee*, OJC) and Elvin Jones (*Motion*), is a tribute to his endurance and invention.

⮑We almost chose **Motion**, Verve, 1998 [1961]

59

Joe Lovano

From The Soul

Blue Note, 1992 (rec. 1991)

Joe Lovano (soprano-sax, alto-sax, tenor-sax), Michel Petrucciani (piano), Dave Holland (bass), Ed Blackwell (drums).

In his late thirties, admired by an increasing coterie of fans and critics for his work in drummer Paul Motian's trio, Joe Lovano became a tenor icon almost overnight. The catalyst turned out to be the quartet led by John Scofield, himself the recent beneficiary of a leap in public esteem (Motian's own apotheosis followed shortly). Lovano's father, a big-toned tenorman often heard battling it out against organ trios, was clearly an influence. Cutting his professional teeth in similar fashion by working with organist Lonnie Smith, Joe Lovano joined Woody Herman's Herd for three years and gigged with the Mel Lewis Orchestra. Grounded solidly in the jazz mainstream, he honed a more adventurous style over several years with Motian.

Albums under his name tend to lean in one or other direction, as standard tunes performed with varying degrees of fidelity to accepted versions rub alongside Lovano's own pieces. This one stands out partly because of an almost perfect balance between restraint and aggression and partly because an all-star quartet – picked "one might think" almost at random – achieves the kind of blend such line-ups don't always manage. If Michel Petrucciani and Dave Holland, regular leaders and virtuoso instrumentalists, grab most attention, Ed Blackwell deserves particular credit for the outcome. Linked to progressive causes since replacing Billy Higgins with Ornette

Coleman in the early 1960s, Blackwell imparts the sense of relaxed ease one associates with musicians from New Orleans, even when conditions may appear to demand something different. His attitude rubs off notably on Holland, who curbs any temptation to overplay and performs with understated elegance.

That describes Holland's introduction to **Fort Worth**, a repetitive theme that, in another context, Lovano might have developed in an agitated manner. With Blackwell laying down a variation on the New Orleans shuffle, the tenorist coaxes notes through a deliciously veiled tone, building to some gently played high harmonics. Lovano swaps his main instrument on three tracks, changing to the alto for **Modern Man**, a duet with Blackwell, who again hints at the shuffle beat, and for John Coltrane's **Central Park West**. The vehicle for one of Coltrane's earliest efforts on soprano, it sounded then, as now, like a cool and quiet "Giant Steps". Lovano stays close to his tenor style, though with his sound less pliable, while Petrucciani can be guaranteed to squeeze the maximum romance from chords such as these. On a lively interpretation (with Blackwell to the fore) of **Work** by Thelonious Monk, Lovano switches to soprano and reminds one of the way Steve Lacy would tackle a Monk tune. It has little in common with any post-Coltrane soprano performance.

The rest feature the tenor. Fairly abstract throughout, but taken at a regular tempo, **Evolution** and the more closely structured **Lines & Spaces** find Lovano stretching out with meticulous control: instead of forcing high notes, he again squeezes them softly. A tenor with his background cannot resist **Body And Soul**. Taken very slowly as a duet with Petrucciani, again in his element, it is packed with harmonic movement that never seems forced. The same two crop up on **Left Behind**, an out-of-tempo ballad, while **Portrait Of Jenny** has excellent solos from piano and bass, framed by Lovano's closest nod to Coltrane on the album.

⮌We almost chose **Rush Hour**, Blue Note, 1995 [1994]

Mahavishnu Orchestra

The Inner Mounting Flame

Columbia, 1998 (rec. 1971)

John McLaughlin ("Mahavishnu") (guitar), Jerry Goodman (violin), Jan Hammer (piano, electric-piano, synth), Rick Laird (electric-bass), Billy Cobham (drums).

During the last thirty-plus years, English-born John McLaughlin has become an honorary American (like Dave Holland or, before either of them, pianist George Shearing). But at the same time he has assimilated so much music and influenced so much of it, from fusion to world-jazz, that he's a truly international figure – quite an achievement for someone who started out playing in "British blues" bands.

Things changed very rapidly for McLaughlin in early 1969. He recorded his debut album (*Extrapolation*, Verve) with a quartet containing John Surman and drummer Tony Oxley, then moved to New York to work with Tony Williams. One month to the day after *Extrapolation*, he played on Miles Davis's *In A Silent Way* session. As well as appearing on several other Davis studio dates, including *Bitches Brew* and the live tracks of *Live-Evil*, the following year McLaughlin taped two more albums under his own name. The second of these (*My Goal's Beyond*) included half an LP's worth of a prototype Mahavishnu Orchestra featuring Jerry Goodman and Billy Cobham, with performances revealing an interest in Indian music and spirituality.

Flamenco guitar was another interest to be explored in greater depth in the future but, by the time McLaughlin formed this band in 1971, his high-speed playing had absorbed all its influences into a seamless and impressive whole. He hired equally virtuosic instrumentalists from a variety of backgrounds, including

Czech-born keyboardist-composer Jan Hammer, Irish bassist Rick Laird, the amplified violin of Goodman and the flamboyant musicality of Cobham, and proceeded to create a stylistic mix that had never been heard before. The energy and the electricity, the decibels and the distortion, clearly came from rock, but the improvisational daring came from jazz, and the thematic material hinted at everything from blues to ragas, all in the same breath.

One thing that distinguished this music from the average rock band, besides its technical accomplishment, was an awareness of textural possibilities and the variation of volume levels. The opening, **Meeting Of The Spirits**, after its heavy fanfare-like chords hammered home by Cobham, begins with a thematic figure starting softly and gradually building in intensity, and the later thickening of lines that suggests overdubbing is actually produced live. The strongest contrast is provided by a totally acoustic trio of guitar, piano and violin on the out-of-tempo **A Lotus On Irish Streams**, whose melody approximates Celtic music played with an Indian sensibility and whose brief decorations constitute the only improvised content. Almost as restrained, **You Know, You Know** is played by the full electric quintet but restricts improvisation to regular breaks at phrase-ends.

There are, of course, connections to McLaughlin's earlier music, such as **The Noonward Race**, which leads off with a riff that he (and Cobham) contributed to Miles's *Jack Johnson* album and later incorporates a figure from "What I Say" on the then-unissued *Live-Evil*. But the high spot has to be **The Dance Of Maya**, one of several tracks that channel the dizzying spirals of McLaughlin's lines into complex time signatures – in this case, 10/4 (or 20/8). The metre is subdivided three different ways for different themes and, when they're finally played simultaneously, it's a moment to make listeners laugh out loud or hug themselves with delight. The fusion-jazz of the early 1970s wasn't noted for its jokes, but this shows that musical humour wasn't entirely lost to view.

↻We almost chose **John McLaughlin – My Goal's Beyond**,

Knit Classics, 1999 [1970]

Branford Marsalis

Requiem

Columbia, 1999 (rec. 1998)

Branford Marsalis (soprano-sax, tenor-sax), Kenny Kirkland (piano), Eric Revis (bass), Jeff "Tain" Watts (drums).

After leaving the Wynton Marsalis quintet, elder brother Branford toured with Sting and later led a jazz-meets-hip-hop group while Wynton delved into the past. Never as close musically as one imagined, and subsequently branching out in opposite directions, there are similarities in that both brothers studied the jazz history of their respective instruments and, even if his main models tend to be of more recent vintage, Branford can still nod in the direction of Ben Webster when he feels the urge.

Two of his favourite musicians, pianist Kenny Kirkland and drummer Jeff "Tain" Watts, were part of the original Wynton Marsalis group. Both joined Branford in the late 1980s and remained his preferred accomplices right up to Kirkland's death in 1998, during the period when this album was recorded – hence the title, **Requiem**. Each reacts positively, as a team or as individuals, to what the saxophonist plays, while the newest member, bassist Eric Revis, takes on more the role of straight man.

Branford Marsalis wrote all but one of the themes. The opening **Doctone** immediately brings Watts to the forefront as he counters Kirkland's solo with a whirl of sticks before slipping into an effortless 4/4 as the pianist hits his second chorus. Drawing from a different arsenal of sound effects, Watts shares with Elvin Jones the priceless knack of conjuring up cross-rhythms that blow your head off while simultaneously ramming home the basic beat, as he does to perfection behind Marsalis on the faster passages of **Trieste** and **Elysium**.

An unintended memorial to Kirkland, the album succeeds in highlighting his qualities. Coming from the lyrical line of post-1960s pianists, he also packs something of McCoy Tyner's punchy attack, noticeable when he cuts loose on "Trieste". Written by drummer Paul Motian in the 1970s, this version switches from a ululating, Arabic-type exposition to uptempo improvising from Kirkland and Marsalis, skimming lightly on soprano as his phrases entwine themselves around the barrage set up by Watts.

Kirkland's rhapsodic side comes to the fore on **Cassandra** and on a couple of tunes that Marsalis had recorded previously with just bass and drums in support. Both **A Thousand Autumns** and **Lykief** are taken enticingly slow, the latter developing as an occasionally frenetic out-of-tempo improvisation, with lots of holes for Watts to fill, on a melody that soprano and piano milk for all it's worth, much as a coloratura queen works up her audience.

Marsalis seems to be moving towards the soprano as his major saxophone voice – in the way one of his idols, Wayne Shorter, did after Weather Report got off the ground. There's a keening quality to his tone as it hangs in the air on ballads – an awareness of Jan Garbarek extends to bits of the tenor solo on "A Thousand Autumns" – though, as "Trieste" and **Bulworth** indicate, Marsalis is equally prepared to take Watts head-on when the drummer kicks. The fluidity of line exemplified on "Doctone" and "Elysium" engenders the kind of frisson one hopes for when top tenors and drummers interact at some pace.

The final track has a brief coda grafted on. Possibly not intended at the time for release, it features an improvised duet between Marsalis (at his most ethereal on soprano) and Kirkland that, under the circumstances, could not have provided a more moving finale.

⊃We almost chose **Crazy People Music**, Columbia, 1990

Wynton Marsalis

Citi Movement

Columbia, 1993 (rec. 1992)

Marsalis (trumpet), Wycliffe Gordon (trombone), Todd Williams (soprano-sax, tenor-sax), Wes Anderson (alto-sax), Herb Harris (tenor-sax), Eric Reed, Marthaniel Roberts (piano), Reginald Veal (bass), Herlin Riley (drums).

Controversy always surrounds jazz people who do something new. Wynton Marsalis raises spirits and hackles in sizable chunks through becoming the first to triumph by looking back. Good enough to win Grammy awards both for jazz and for European classics, he played with Art Blakey's Jazz Messengers and then led a group based loosely on Miles Davis's 1960s quintet. His next tie-up should logically have been with electric guitars, perhaps, or the Third World: instead, he formed a septet that resembled a Duke Ellington small band, symbolized by Marsalis and trombonist Wycliffe Gordon carrying between them about a dozen mutes.

Given his reputation as a trumpeter first and foremost, the way Marsalis reintroduced US audiences to the jazz ensemble as a vehicle for scores of surpassing complexity – all of which he wrote himself – came as a shock. Heavily involved at the time in recreating the classics of (especially) Ellington, he adapted many of their conventions and came up with something personal. **Citi Movement**, a double album recorded in 1992, had been commissioned for a ballet. Marsalis begins **Hustle Bustle**, opening movement of the kaleidoscopic **Cityscape**, with simulated traffic noises, just as Jelly Roll Morton began his "Sidewalk Blues". **City Beat** ticks over smoothly in the Ellington manner before switching to a Latin section, underlining programmatic links between "Cityscape" and the Duke's

"Harlem Suite". However, the detail of the writing differs: for instance, Ellington rarely got instruments or time signatures to zig-zag as they do on parts of "City Beat" and **Stop And Go**.

The second of the three suites, **Transatlantic Echoes**, looks at older traditions and how they might relate to jazz. One expects blues and church music, but there's also a mock-Viennese waltz, while the New Orleans/Caribbean ethos of **Bayou Baroque** is ruffled by rhythms resembling those of East European dances. Jazz history of a sort inspired **Some Present Moments Of The Future**, encapsulated by the opening **The End** – mostly Dixieland until a final spatter of free blowing.

Improvisation entwined with ensemble virtuosity, a combination mainstream jazz had not experienced at this level since the Modern Jazz Quartet, was carried out by mostly little-known youngsters Marsalis met on his travels. Including, of course, the leader, they have New Orleans or Deep South connections, evident in their collectively relaxed approach. A towering figure throughout, Wycliffe Gordon appears to run the gamut of Ellington effects, except that the guttural rasps on "Stop And Go" and the svelte phrasing on **Nightlife Highlife** are his own and not lifted wholesale from Tricky Sam Nanton or Lawrence Brown. Wes Anderson's solos always hold plenty in reserve, while his creamy sound fits this kind of music perfectly.

Having applied the same single-mindedness he once dedicated to mastering the trumpet in teaching himself the art of orchestration, Marsalis's writing often imparts a similar feeling of exuberance. He knows how to cool it, however, as on the delicious **Marthaniel**, a boogie crawling at just above funeral pace and largely a solo by Marthaniel (Marcus) Roberts. Trumpet features are few but astounding. Marsalis squeezes every emotional drop from **Spring Yaoundé**. His brand of majesty on the king of jazz instruments is exemplified on this slow waltz by some high-note sequences and by the grandstanding coda, passages only he could conceive. The groovier tempo of **Modern Vistas** inspires a very model of the modern blues solo.

⮑We almost chose **Live At Blues Alley**, Columbia, 1988 [1986]

63

Pat Metheny

80/81

ECM, undated (rec. 1980)

Metheny (guitar), Mike Brecker, Dewey Redman (tenor-sax), Charlie Haden (bass),
Jack DeJohnette (drums).

From his early appearances aged nineteen in Gary Burton's quartet, listeners have tended to categorize Pat Metheny as purveying what is variously described as jazz-fusion or jazz-rock. If not totally misleading when judged by the bulk of his output, that description hardly does justice to possibly the most versatile guitarist around, in terms of the different instruments he uses and the contexts in which these are deployed, ranging from free-form to the heaviest thrash. The side of him reflecting his apprenticeship as a fan of Wes Montgomery has come more to the forefront, and this side lies uppermost on the double album **80/81**.

Eight tracks split the quintet several ways. A couple are by guitar, bass and drums plus Mike Brecker, and these throw up many of the highlights. Not immediately acknowledged as a major figure, Brecker's ultra-fluent technique proved an irresistible magnet for a younger generation of tenor saxophonists. When allied to a penetrating sound, somewhat gravelly in the manner of latter-day Sonny Rollins, his example offered an alternative to the prevailing influence of John Coltrane.

Brecker stars on the first section of **Two Folk Songs**, striding through Metheny's theme against a rock-like rhythm and then improvising around one of those two-chord harmonic bases that, by the 1980s, were squeezing out modal forms. Over DeJohnette's increasingly proactive beat, the outlines somewhat resemble those found during a typical Rollins Caribbean-type solo, though Brecker's effortless switch between high and low registers at speed, and the occasional leap to the stratosphere, impose their own identity. He takes the process further during a coda in which the post-Ayler cries grow more intense. The second theme is played at a slower tempo by composer Charlie Haden, followed by a solo whose deep tones and relaxed strumming are a trademark. Imparting a faint country twang that fits the ambience, Metheny's single lines develop into a chordal passage before his strumming takes it out.

A charge pundits hurl against Metheny is that – apart from acknowledged exceptions, notably the increasing echoes of Ornette Coleman – his preferred musical settings have a soft centre. **Every Day (I Thank You)** resembles a rock ballad and, at this slow tempo, with Metheny's sitar-plus-synthesizer effects, the mood grows a trifle glutinous, but Brecker's sheer bravado as he roars through the registers while notes flash by imposes a sense of grandeur, even if over the top. The other ballad, **The Bat**, is pretty without being mawkish and has movingly restrained solos from Metheny and Haden.

For Ornette Coleman's influence on Metheny's composing, one need not look beyond the title tune, performed by a quartet containing, in Dewey Redman and Charlie Haden, two ex-Coleman regulars. Here, and on the equally pacy **Turnaround**, a Coleman twelve-bar blues, Metheny picks superbly at speed like a cool guitarist, but one with a tangy edge. What strikes home especially are the supple rhythmic variations as his notes flow and tumble across the beat, giving a balalaika effect notably on "Turnaround". Another blues, **Pretty Scattered**, gets progressively freer as DeJohnette loosens the tempo behind Metheny, though the collective interplay by all members on **Open** adds little to what people did more convincingly in the 1960s. There's a Latin lilt to the folksy **Goin' Ahead**, just Metheny duetting with himself on acoustic guitar.

⊃We almost chose **Trio Live**, Warner 2000, [1999–2000]

64

Charles Mingus

Blues & Roots

Atlantic, 1998 (rec. 1959)

Mingus (bass), Jimmy Knepper, Willie Dennis (trombone), Jackie McLean, John Handy (alto-sax), Booker Ervin (tenor-sax), Pepper Adams (baritone-sax), Horace Parlan, Mal Waldron (piano), Dannie Richmond (drums).

Mingus can be somewhat intimidating and there's a category of fans who find that, as with Ellington and perhaps Monk, he stands outside their view of jazz history. But once you get to know him, he's impossible to ignore and, for many listeners, this leads to a lifelong love affair. Again, as with Ellington, Mingus's music comes in many shapes and sizes and, though there are always characteristic touches identifying the composer, it's impossible to summarize his output by choosing a single album.

Nevertheless, there are people who get hooked on Mingus at first hearing, and it often turns out that they are aficionados of blues bands and gospel music. Not only were these a part of Mingus's background but the emotional directness of such African-American roots music is a fundamental aspect of his appeal. An earlier epoch-making album, the 1956 *Pithecanthropus Erectus* (Atlantic), can be seen as a mix of r&b, gospel and "modal jazz" – before it acquired the name – and marked a complete about-turn from the Europeanized approaches of the Modern Jazz Quartet or Lennie Tristano, who had previously influenced Mingus's thinking. So, after sessions touching on speech-and-jazz (*The Clown, Scenes In The City*) or Mexican-music-and-jazz (*Tijuana Moods*), it was a stroke of genius for producer Nesuhi Ertegun to request a Mingus collection concentrating on the blues.

The bassist jumped at the chance and assembled a nine-piece band combining his current quintet with other recent sidemen, and expanded on the methods he'd developed with them. Avoiding written music and communicating his themes orally, he created ensemble passages with simultaneous themes on different instruments and encouraged (even demanded) participation in each other's improvised solos. The classic opener, **Wednesday Night Prayer Meeting**, has his bass introduction and the solos of Handy and Dennis supported by other horn players "feeling the spirit", while Parlan's funky piano is nearly drowned out by ensemble riffs more basic than anything in the Swing era. More strikingly, Ervin's hoarse "preaching" tenor finds the rhythm-section breaking off and replaced by congregational clapping – an effect endlessly copied on pop records.

Three of the six tracks are based on the twelve-bar blues and show the inherent versatility of the form: "Prayer Meeting", the organized chaos of **E's Flat, Ah's Flat Too** and the slow field-holler of **Cryin' Blues** featuring a raw solo by Jackie McLean. Two more use similar techniques over longer forms betraying a lingering trace of bebop, **Tensions** and **Moanin'** – the latter not to be confused with Bobby Timmons's tune for Art Blakey, now famous in the UK for its use in a television advert. Exemplifying the breadth of Mingus's interest in, and playing experience with, elders such as Louis Armstrong, **My Jelly Roll Soul** is his affectionate tribute to the famous Morton and, against the odds, combines a trad-jazz influence with current improvising styles.

Two other albums, *Mingus Ah Um* (1959) and *The Black Saint And The Sinner Lady* (1963), deserve a special mention. Unlike *Blues And Roots*, they each contain a couple of his highly distinctive ballads (including, in the case of *Ah Um*, his biggest hit, "Goodbye Pork Pie Hat"), while *Ah Um* also has two tunes that are alternative approaches to the same material as "Prayer Meeting" and "Jelly Roll Soul" on **Blues And Roots**. But, if you want to know why blues freaks fall for Mingus, or if you simply want your life never to be the same again, this is the place to start.

⮑We almost chose **Mingus Ah Um**, Columbia, 1998 [1959]

65

Modern Jazz Quartet

Django

OJC, 1987 (rec. 1953–55)

Milt Jackson (vibraphone), John Lewis (piano), Percy Heath (bass), Kenny Clarke (drums).

The MJQ were one of the longest-surviving groups in the whole of jazz history, starting life as the rhythm-section and mid-set intermission group of the late 1940s Dizzy Gillespie big band, when Ray Brown was their bassist. They made their first quartet records under Jackson's name in 1948 (included on *In The Beginning*, OJC) and again for Gillespie's label in 1951–52 (*The Quartet*, Savoy). But it was not until Jackson signed with Prestige later in 1952 that recordings initially billed as the "Milt Jackson Modern Jazz Quartet" led to the musical developments with which their name is associated.

What was different from this point on was that pianist John Lewis (a former colleague of both Charlie Parker and Miles Davis as well as Gillespie) began asserting himself as the quartet's musical director, a title he adopted officially when the group became a touring unit. His previous compositions for Dizzy and Miles had betrayed a considerable interest in the techniques of European music and, with a piano style that often made the instrument sound more like a harpsichord, he saw that combining it with vibes could create unique results, if carefully arranged. The precarious balance between his planning and the freely improvised bebop-and-blues-based blowing of Jackson lent the group a creative tension that reached a surprisingly wide audience.

While there are no out-and-out jazz fugues here (such as the contemporaneous *Concorde* album's title track and "Vendome")

Lewis manages to incorporate bits of written counterpoint into his versions of a couple of standards and the originals **Milano**, **Delaunay's Dilemma** and **The Queen's Fancy**. (His love affair with things European is revealed by these tune titles, the second-named referring to French discographer/record producer Charles Delaunay, while the third was recorded in the same month as the coronation of England's Elizabeth II.) Nevertheless, "Milano" is actually a melody he first composed for Miles Davis and Tadd Dameron, "Fancy" is a baroque rewrite of "Rouge" (done for Davis's *Birth Of The Cool* band) and the **La Ronde Suite** consists of four variations on "Two Bass Hit", a Lewis number recorded by both Gillespie (*Complete RCA Victor Recordings*) and Davis (*Milestones*).

The MJQ versions are invariably more restrained than those of others, but they are often filled with fascinating details, such as a non-blues twelve-bar section in the middle of "Fancy" or the six-bar interlude on "Dilemma". Originally the lead-track of the first album credited to the Modern Jazz Quartet, the seven-minute **Django** (a memorial to French guitarist Django Reinhardt, who died the previous year), also has an unusual structure, plus an unexpected interlude between the evocative solos by Jackson and Lewis (the latter played almost entirely in chords). Though its initial appearance provoked cries of "Is it jazz?", this is one of the Quartet's most moving pieces.

A further reminder of the group's feet in different camps is that, at 7:50 of "La Ronde Suite", Jackson blithely quotes "Epistrophy" by Thelonious Monk, with whom he had also recorded successfully in recent years. (More extraordinary, perhaps, is the fact that a two-bar extract at 2:45 of the same track is sampled on Branford Marsalis's album *Buckshot La Fonque*). Although the driving drumming of Kenny Clarke was replaced in 1955 by Connie Kay, the Quartet's career lasted into the 1990s and it's only a shame that two excellent live albums, *The European Concert* and *Dedicated To Connie* (both Atlantic) seem to be currently unavailable.

⮩We almost chose **Concorde**, OJC, 1987 [1952–55]

66

Thelonious Monk

Brilliant Corners

OJC, 1987 (rec. 1956)

Monk (piano), Clark Terry (trumpet), Ernie Henry (alto-sax), Sonny Rollins (tenor-sax), Oscar Pettiford, Paul Chambers (bass), Max Roach (drums).

Nearly twenty years after his death, Thelonious Monk can still be a controversial performer for some listeners. In the past, Oscar Peterson and others put him down for his lack of conventional pianistic ability; yet, as Bill Evans said, "They somehow feel he's eccentric, but Monk knows exactly what he's doing … structurally, and musically, he's aware of every note he plays." For a while Thelonious became more famous for his hats than his playing but, now that the fame has worn off somewhat, his captivating music has to win the argument, and it's more than adequate to the task.

Many of the players who follow Monk's example, in terms of his unusual note choices and highly percussive touch, are people who also revere the piano work of Duke Ellington (who was far from a conventional executant himself). Despite differences of style and personality, both Ellington and Monk are interested in sonorities, in compositional forms and in having their musicians interpret the mood of a piece, rather than just its chord changes. Thelonious was not always so lucky as the Duke in that respect – perhaps because he only had a regular working personnel from 1957 to about 1970 – and even his classic early Blue Note records (collected on *Genius Of Modern Music Vols 1 and 2* and excerpted on *The Best Of*) feature few fully sympathetic sidemen apart from Milt Jackson and Art Blakey.

While many of Monk's most absorbing recordings feature his piano either in a trio setting or totally solo, **Brilliant Corners** represents a triumph among his performances with hornmen (though including an unaccompanied version of the standard, **I Surrender Dear**). Rollins, who appears throughout the rest, was a member of Max Roach's band at the time but worked with Monk on several occasions, even employing him as a sideman on two of his own records; Sonny's ability to tear the meat off a piece and get to the marrow is never more apparent than on Monk compositions. The less well-known Ernie Henry was to die prematurely a year later, but does some of his best work on the two pieces on which he solos. The most surprising choice at the time seemed to be Ellington trumpeter Clark Terry, who is by no means misplaced on the one track he graces and also went on to use Monk on his own album.

Bemsha Swing, the early Monk tune co-written with drummer Denzil Best, is a lively but unsettling rendition with Terry, Roach punctuating on timpani(!) and Rollins quoting twice from Bud Powell's "Un Poco Loco". The long and bumpy twelve-bar, **Ba-Lue Bolivar Ba-Lues-Are**, and the typical Monk ballad, **Pannonica**, both have searching solos by Rollins and the latter an excursion from the leader on celeste. (Use of the timpani and celeste by less heavyweight musicians would seem gimmicky, but there's no danger of that here.) The opening title track is the *pièce de résistance*, however, its seemingly threatening theme difficult to play and its solo structure presenting huge hurdles, but all involved (including Roach) make perfect sense of it.

By the way, it's been mentioned in at least one other publication that "Pannonica", as heard on all issues to date, suffers from the tape machine employed running too fast initially and gradually achieving the correct speed after thirty seconds (so the playback starts too slow and speeds up). Please, can this be corrected when the time comes for the next remastering?

⮑ We almost chose **The Best Of Thelonious Monk**,

Blue Note, 1990 [1947–52]

67

Wes Montgomery

The Incredible Jazz Guitar Of Wes Montgomery

OJC, 1987 (rec. 1960)

Montgomery (guitar), Tommy Flanagan (piano), Percy Heath (bass), Albert Heath (drums).

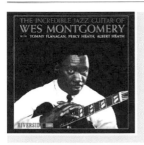

The start of 1960 saw Ornette Coleman settling into his first extended New York residency at the Five Spot, and Charles Mingus inaugurating one of his most radical groups at the Spotlite. Not long after, Cecil Taylor added saxophonist Archie Shepp to his trio and John Coltrane launched his famous quartet, which in the autumn was briefly augmented by two further musicians, Eric Dolphy and Wes Montgomery. Though underlining Wes's wide-open ears and all-encompassing technique, the latter choice was a surprise because he had just begun to establish himself as a leader of mainstream post-bop jazz.

Montgomery was in fact the person who made the contemporary jazz world safe for guitarists again. Since the bebop movement of fifteen years earlier, the instrument risked being pushed to the sidelines, despite the laudable efforts of players such as Jimmy Raney and Tal Farlow, and instead it seemed to have found its natural home in rock'n'roll. Wes ignored the latter tendency (unlike Kenny Burrell and Grant Green, who occasionally flirted with it), while nevertheless looking back to Charlie Christian and emphasizing the blues inheritance of the best jazz improvisers. He also showed the breadth of his knowledge by incorporating the skilfully voiced four-note chords of Barney Kessel and the use of open octaves pioneered by Django Reinhardt.

Prior to the late 1950s, Montgomery had spent most of his time in his native Indianapolis, working at a day job and playing most of the night to support a large family. His only previous releases, apart from an almost invisible stint with Lionel Hampton, were two for Pacific Jazz involving an association with his siblings (pianist-vibist Buddy and bassist Monk Montgomery) and one for Riverside with his Indianapolis-based organ trio. The impact of this first set with a driving New York rhythm-section was therefore exceptional, especially as he was clearly leading them, rather than vice versa. The longest track, **West Coast Blues**, in 6/4, is full of unstoppable invention as well as technically amazing, and the slower **D-Natural Blues** leads so effortlessly into double time that the rhythm-section is eventually dragged along too.

The other two original numbers were both in the then-fashionable minor key, the lightly Latin **Mr Walker** and the loping **Four On Six** (based on Montgomery's bass-line to "Summertime" from the 1958–59 Pacific Jazz album *Far Wes*). They inspire lengthy solos from the leader and shorter ones from a superbly on-form Tommy Flanagan, as do Sonny Rollins's **Airegin** and Dave Brubeck's **In Your Own Sweet Way**. There is evidence of editing on the latter (and in the abnormally short drum solo of "Four On Six"), presumably to place greater emphasis on the guitarist, but his supremely logical development of the medium-tempo standard **Gone With The Wind** shows him carrying the whole show.

Wes's punishing work schedule in the period preceding his late 1950s discovery may have contributed to his premature death, but the understandable desire for an easier life led to a stifling of creativity in his last few years. His role as the godfather of what became "smooth jazz" was well established by the limited invention on some of his big-band recordings and especially those with strings, which were all about playing the tune and nothing else. By comparison, his playing here is wholly credible (contrary to the album title) and the inherent melodicism of his improvisations – which has been compared to that of Louis Armstrong – effortlessly stands the test of time.

⮑We almost chose **Full House**, OJC, 1987 [1962]

Lee Morgan

Cornbread

Blue Note, 1988 (rec. 1965)

Morgan (trumpet), Jackie McLean (alto-sax), Hank Mobley (tenor-sax), Herbie Hancock (piano), Larry Ridley (bass), Billy Higgins (drums).

Lee Morgan enlivened the jazz world from an early age, joining the Dizzy Gillespie band in autumn 1956 (when he was eighteen) and making the first of his many recordings in the same year. His command of the instrument and his puckish sense of humour marked an individual take on the style of Clifford Brown, whose demise preceded Morgan's emergence on the national scene by a mere few months, but his playing also incorporated the squeezed-note half-valve effects of trumpeters such as Rex Stewart and Clark Terry. In addition, it accommodated a great empathy for blues phraseology, which made him a highly appropriate choice to play in Art Blakey's Jazz Messengers, whom he first joined in 1958.

He had just left the band for the second time when he made the **Cornbread** album. In the meantime, an earlier Blue Note disc, titled after its lead tune "The Sidewinder", achieved a remarkable sales success through jukebox and radio play, and its later use in a television commercial. The funk allusions of the bass-line combined with a melody poised between r&b and hard-bop to generate a momentum that was less of an influence on Morgan himself than on the record label. Firstly, it enabled Blue Note to finance sessions by more avant-garde musicians (in many cases still selling today, but at the time not expected to recoup their costs quickly) and it more or less obliged their more conventional albums henceforth to lead off with a similarly catchy ditty.

In this instance **Cornbread**, as its title implies, is much more downhome in intent than "Sidewinder" – its triadic harmony from the three horns, its AABA sixteen-bar approach extended by four bars each chorus, and especially its two-bar breaks in the theme recall both 1920s jazz and country-blues. To show that he's not hampered by any formula, Morgan injects a considerable amount of variety into the remainder of his compositions. **Our Man Higgins** is a fast 24-bar blues featuring breaks by the drummer, with the whole-tone-scale implications of its melody duly taken up in the solos. For a further contrast, **Ceora** (now something of a standard) is a unique species of bebop bossa nova whose laidback feel is set up by the 32-bar-long introduction from Hancock and the rhythm-section, while **Most Like Lee** is close to the early hard-bop Morgan was involved in nearly a decade before.

Throughout this original material, the trumpeter's playing is consistently alive and inventive, and on the Harold Arlen ballad **Ill Wind** he differentiates his sound from the conventional Miles Davis-patented harmon-mute with the stem removed, by leaving the stem in (again, the effect is to hark back to earlier styles). Mobley, who recorded many sessions with Morgan, is close to his best form, on "Our Man" quoting Coltrane's "Some Other Blues", while Lee quotes Charlie Parker's solo from "Billie's Bounce". The seasoning is provided by McLean, soloing on three out of five tracks and deterring the others from any hint of complacency. Hancock, as often in this period, is in a more straight-ahead setting than when working with Miles, but enlivens each piece by getting truly involved in the implications of the material.

Morgan is close to being a perfect example of the kind of widely recorded artist whose albums are always a reliable bet and therefore uniformly recommendable. But this example, while it has its fans, should be far better known.

⮑We almost chose **The Sidewinder**, Blue Note, 1999 [1963]

69

Jelly Roll Morton

The Original Mr Jelly Lord 1923–1941

Avid, 2000 (rec. 1923–40)

Morton (piano, vocals, leader), with various groups including his Jazz Band and Orchestra, St. Louis Levee Band, Red Hot Peppers, Levee Serenaders, Trio, New Orleans Jazzmen, Seven.

In his fine sleeve-note accompanying this essential set, Morton authority Martin Litton quotes clarinettist Barney Bigard. "Up until he died (in July 1941), I think Jelly was above Ellington, but as the years progressed Ellington surpassed him. I think Jelly wrote more damn tunes than Ellington ever thought about writing. All I can say is I think Jelly is one of the greatest, and he should be in the Hall of Fame."

It's a fascinating triple statement, and certainly true in part. During their concurrent recording years (1924–30) Morton's output, though very different, was creatively comparable to Ellington's. Far more questionable, however, is Bigard's qualification "up until he died". For almost all of the 1930s, while Ellington surged ahead, Morton was inactive, returning only for final recording sessions, in a broad New Orleans format between 1939 and 1940, just as Ellington was about to embark on his incomparable "Blanton-Webster" period with an orchestra ready to answer the call.

No matter. Morton's technicolour career as pianist-composer-bandleader stands firmly on its own – the result of a highly original musical mind, and the ability to put his thoughts into notes. He was a more-than-capable pianist (who was probably recording piano rolls as early as 1915), a deeply original composer operating at what would now be called the cutting edge of his music, and a skilled orchestrator with an ear for detail in both conception and realization of his aims. His best-known sides are unquestionably with his Red Hot Peppers, and **The Original Mr Jelly Lord 1923–1941** is an admirable collection collating all their sides in chronological order, with crystal-clear sound restoration from Dave Bennett.

Morton always rehearsed thoroughly before recording and his note-perfect results shine out on acknowledged classics like Mel Stitzel's modernistic **The Chant**, the Spanish-tinged **Original Jelly Roll Blues** and the majestically themed **Grandpa's Spells** and **Pearls** (proof enough that at this time Morton was running Ellington close to the fence). One difference between them was Morton's weighty humour, which introduces mini-sketches before **Sidewalk Blues**, **Dead Man Blues** and **Steamboat Stomp**, plus real vaudeville elsewhere: farmyard imitations on **Billy Goat Stomp**, and laughter on **Hyena Stomp**, which consequently falls somewhere between Slim Gaillard's "Laughin In Rhythm" and "The Laughing Policeman" (ostensibly not written until 1938, incidentally!). Such additives (as well as a **Wild Man Blues**, recorded one month after Louis Armstrong's towering version with his Hot Seven, but lacking most of the majesty) suggest that Morton wasn't taking himself seriously, but sanity is restored with the 1928 Red Hot Peppers' titles, which include **Georgia Swing** and **Kansas City Stomps**.

While slightly less famous, Morton's later sides are regularly of priceless value. **Deep Creek** (from 1928) – which for the first time presents Morton as aspiring big-band leader – is described by fellow annotator and consummate authority Brian Rust as "one of the most absolute jazz masterpieces of all time". Both Rust and Litton draw attention to the Morton trio dates of 1929 (with Bigard and Zutty Singleton), pointing out that they pre-date Benny Goodman's Trio by five years, and two of Morton's four piano solos from the same year (**Seattle Hunch** and **Freakish**) are here too. So is a fair proportion of his remaining discography (including six of his final sides from 1939), completing a superbly scholastic and satisfying reissue of Morton music.

➲No alternative – **a truly comprehensive album**

70

Gerry Mulligan

The Best Of The Gerry Mulligan Quartet With Chet Baker

Pacific Jazz, 1991 (rec. 1952–57)

Mulligan (baritone-sax), Chet Baker (trumpet), Bobby Whitlock, Carson Smith, Henry Grimes (bass), Chico Hamilton, Larry Bunker, Dave Bailey (drums).

Like many who experience fame early in life, Mulligan had a rather episodic career. The same is even more true of Chet Baker, his partner in this celebrated group, although it's arguable that Baker really found his niche much later on. Mulligan oscillated regularly between his interest in writing for larger ensembles, with streamlined subtlety and a light-hearted feel, and his ease in playing a notoriously awkward instrument.

His saxophone had already been heard on a small number of small-group sessions, revealing an ability to adapt the prevailing Lester Young-derived style to the baritone, and with particular success on the Miles Davis nonet recordings later called *The Birth Of The Cool*. His original compositions for that group were, along with the writing of Gil Evans, one of the band's defining elements, and indeed one quartet tune here was a new version of the *TBOTC* piece **Jeru**. But what was strikingly different was the stripped-down line-up of just two horns and the consequent removal of Mulligan's arranged voicings, compounded by the absence of any chordal backing from either piano or guitar.

The first important pianoless (and drumless) quartet was probably the Sidney Bechet-Muggsy Spanier Big Four, convened for just two studio sessions in 1940, but even this had a rhythm guitar to spell out the harmonic foundation. Later, the trio, led in

1950–51 by vibraphonist Red Norvo, similarly omitted piano and drums, but had guitarist Tal Farlow contributing both melody and chords. These early "chamber-jazz" groups had a significant influence on several new developments. Norvo, in fact, did so in the most practical manner possible, since the piano that was put into storage during his six nights a week at the Haig Club in Los Angeles was the same piano that Mulligan was unable to use on Norvo's night off.

Having discovered his new line-up and an instinctive improviser in Baker, Mulligan was immediately recorded for a new label and achieved instant celebrity with catchy singles such as **Bernie's Tune**, **Nights At The Turntable** and the widely covered **Walkin' Shoes**. To flesh out the sparse group sound, the bass-lines of these tunes were carefully arranged to provide a third harmony part, while Mulligan and Baker filled in more spontaneously behind each other's solos, occasionally stretching to a kind of neo-Dixieland joint improvisation. Within a few months of their early hits, a couple of ballads have off-mike vocal harmonies(!) as occasional backgrounds, while **I'm Beginning To See The Light** is played with rather sardonic humour. There's no knowing how the group would have developed, since it broke up after less than a year and Baker went off to found his own career on the success of the quartet's **My Funny Valentine** (included here in an impressive live version).

The final track is from a reunion whereby Baker replaced Mulligan's then-trumpeter Art Farmer, heard to great effect on the deleted Columbia album *What Is There To Say?* The baritonist, meanwhile, became involved in all-star sessions and eventually launched a twelve-piece band (which he reconvened sporadically into the 1990s), an early blueprint for which is included in the album *Mullenium*. The jury may still be out on where Mulligan's huge talent fits, and whether he ever used it to the full, but meanwhile this music helped to define "cool jazz" far more than the Davis band did. Far from just a handy time capsule, it still sounds remarkably fresh today.

⮑ We almost chose **Mullenium**, Columbia, 1998 [1946–57]

71

David Murray

Ming

Black Saint, 1994 (rec. 1980)

Murray (tenor-sax, bass-clarinet), Henry Threadgill (alto-sax), Olu Dara (trumpet), Lawrence "Butch" Morris (cornet), George Lewis (trombone), Anthony Davis (piano), Wilber Morris (bass), Steve McCall (drums).

In his prime, David Murray was hailed by many critics as the next major figure in jazz. The twenty-year-old wunderkind appeared suddenly on New York's so called "loft scene" in 1975 from his first port of call in southern California, and made a mark almost immediately with a series of stunning group records, such as *3-D Family* (hat Hut) with South African bassist Johnny Dyani and drummer Andrew Cyrille, *Live At The Lower Manhattan Ocean Club* (two LPs on India Navigation) with trumpeter Lester Bowie, and the glorious *Flowers For Albert* (India Navigation), dedicated to early saxophone influence Albert Ayler. Murray joined forces with Julius Hemphill, Oliver Lake and Hamiet Bluiett to form the World Saxophone Quartet, and he was even audacious enough, right off the bat, to offer three records of solo tenor and bass-clarinet music, giving the world a glimpse of the huge talent straining to get out of his horn.

Like many creative jazz musicians of the era, Murray found most of the outlets for documentation in Europe, and his most fruitful relationship was with the Italian Black Saint label, who issued some small-group and big-band records, as well as his crowning achievement, the pair of early 1980s octet records, **Ming** and *Home*. With a line-up that included some of the most important and innovative figures of the period – Henry Threadgill, Steve McCall and George Lewis from Chicago's AACM, outstanding pianist and composer Anthony Davis, slippery blues trumpeter Olu Dara, and long-term Murray compadre Butch Morris – this ensemble was a veritable post-free-jazz supergroup, but one in which the music lived up to the hype. Playing all his own pieces, steeped in Mingus (dramatic themes set in sectional forms), Ornette (structured free play, sometimes over swing rhythm, without cycles of changes), and New Orleans (improvised heterophony), Murray was a forceful, original composer and arranger.

By accenting it two different ways, he turns a single melody from a scampering Ornettish line into a bawdy blues on **Dewey's Circle**. McCall's backroom 4/4 is infectious, creating a magnetic pocket that draws great solos from the brass. **The Fast Life** could be a tone poem on NYC – bustling, layered, full of contrasting motion, with a frantic fractured-bop head arranged like a small big band. Murray's supercharged solo contains dynamic, punchy tonguing, and Morris's solo shows what a great player he was; he now spends most of his time focused on "conductions" (improvised conducting) which have been documented on several celebrated multi-disc boxes. **The Hill** starts as a sombre, dark meditation, Wilber Morris's bowed bass underlining Butch's minimalist textures and Murray's characteristic registral leaps on bass clarinet; it shifts gears into a lushly voiced section, gradually more dense and free, climaxing in a radiant orchestrated outro. Threadgill and McCall lock in on one another immaculately here, which makes sense since, together with bassist Fred Hopkins, they constituted Air, one of the greatest trios of new jazz. George Lewis's unearthly trombone is spotlit on the ballad **Ming** – he shares the caressing melody with Threadgill – and Lewis is also monstrous on **Jasvan**, a bright, almost showy waltz with concise solos for all.

Somewhere at the start of the 1990s, Murray lost some of his spark. He's still a powerhouse player, but, where the fire and drive of his titanic tenor carried over into a multi-dimensional musical concept, now he seems content to play out his days, making scads of records – none nearly as interesting as this one – as a journeyman saxophonist.

↪We almost chose **Flowers For Albert**, India Navigation, 1997 [1976]

72

King Oliver

King Oliver's Creole Jazz Band: The Complete Set!

Retrieval, 1996 (rec. 1923–24)

Oliver, Louis Armstrong (cornet), Honore Dutrey, Eddie Atkins (trombone), Johnny Dodds, Paul "Stump" Evans, Jimmy Noone, Buster Bailey, Charlie Jackson (reeds), Lillian Hardin, Clarence Williams, Jelly Roll Morton (piano), Bill Johnson, Johnny St Cyr (banjo), Warren "Baby" Dodds (drums).

Unquestionably one of the music's greatest ensembles, King Oliver's Creole Jazz Band also represents a unique watershed – the crucial bridging point between jazz as an ensemble music and a fully fledged soloist's art form. Within its ranks, dramatically enough, were the two leaders who could be said to personify the changeover – cornettists King Oliver and his young protégé, Louis Armstrong. Oliver's proud title had been won in New Orleans with Kid Ory's band and he was a fine player, skilled with mutes – "the greatest freak trumpet player I ever knew," said contemporary Mutt Carey. But, after hearing the younger Armstrong tearing up the town, Oliver invited his young pupil and friend into the Creole Jazz Band to play second cornet against his own lead. And this Armstrong willingly did, until his new partner (pianist Lil Hardin) warned Louis that "It's Poppa Joe or me. I don't want to be married to no second trumpet player!" Armstrong left, and changed the course of jazz forever.

While the Creole Jazz Band was together it was a proud zenith for New Orleans music and an inspiration for legions of youthful jazz followers later to become stars in their own right. The unbeatable two-cornet team of Oliver and Armstrong was paced by the passionate clarinet of Johnny Dodds (another New Orleans émigré) and trombonist Honore Dutrey; the rhythm-section, as well as Hardin, included Bud Scott and later Johnny St. Cyr (banjo) and was powered by the spectacular rolling drums of Baby Dodds. "That band just went mad when they played", recalled trombonist Preston Jackson. "Usually fast stuff, the Garden was in a turmoil and a tumult from the start of the evening until the last note died away! Especially after Louis Armstrong joined." Armstrong and Oliver's two-part cornet breaks and passages – apparently played from out of the blue – regularly helped to bring the crowd to its feet.

This definitive reissue, **The Complete Set!**, answers a long-felt need. Every title by the Creole Jazz Band is included (with alternate takes), plus four bonus tracks featuring Oliver (two with Butterbeans and Susie, two with Jelly Roll Morton), and all are magnificent. One of the problems with listening to Oliver's music is its unalterable location amid the pre-electric era of sound recording, but the ever-reliable judgment and skill of John R. T. Davies has been brought to bear on a difficult subject and triumphs as always. There are a great many immutable jazz monuments here, among them **Buddy's Habits** and **Snake Rag** (with Armstrong and Oliver's dual skills, and wondrous breaks coming thick and fast); Johnny Dodds's shining on **Room Rent Blues** and **Sweet Lovin' Man** (with Oliver's tearful muted calls), and the stately **Riverside Blues** with Armstrong's first solo on record. Oliver and Armstrong's duo on **Sobbin' Blues** catches the ear too, as does their casual whole-tone sign-off on **Where Did You Stay Last Night**, and the ecstatic **Dippermouth Blues**, of course, has the leader's three ecstatic (and now repertorial) choruses.

There are many substantial compositions spread through the set too, including Oliver's own beautifully conceived and scored **Workin' Man Blues** and almost operatic **Mabel's Dream** by Ike Smith. The Creole Jazz Band, of course, sounded best of all playing live. "They would knock everybody out with about forty minutes of **High Society**", remembered drummer George Wettling. "And then, Joe would look down at me, wink, and then say 'Hotter than a forty five!'." Much of the heat remains on the records, too.

⮌No alternative **– by far the best set available**

73

Charlie Parker

The Dial Masters – Original Choice Takes

Spotlite, 1995 (rec. 1946–47)

Parker (alto-sax), including Miles Davis, Howard McGhee (trumpet), J.J. Johnson (trombone), Lucky Thompson, Wardell Gray (tenor-sax), Dodo Marmarosa, Erroll Garner, Duke Jordan (piano), Red Callender, Tommy Potter (bass), Max Roach (drums), Earl Coleman (vocals).

Miles Davis once said that the history of jazz can be summed up in four words, "Louis Armstrong, Charlie Parker". Though Miles himself seemed to deviate from that belief later, there's a sense in which all the jazz of the past half-century has flowed from the playing of Parker. Complex harmonies or the absence of harmony, complex rhythms in front line or rhythm-section, and the wide variety of possible instrumentation (including strings, woodwind or additional percussion) – all were predicted by and implicit in Bird's innovations.

Yet, like Dizzy Gillespie – who, at the time of the bebop "revolution", was generally seen as its leader – Parker had deep roots in the swing era. Particularly enamoured of Lester Young, he wedded Young's freedom in using the materials of the day to an un-Lestorian virtuosity and volubility that, if anything, suggested the Art Tatum of the saxophone. His early recordings in swing contexts with the Jay McShann band (and small groups led by Tiny Grimes, Clyde Hart, Red Norvo and Slim Gaillard) gained him some fans, but it was the pioneering bebop format – with and without Gillespie – that really showed what Parker was capable of.

A considerable amount of material was cut between 1945 and 1948, all of it important. Although many crucial tracks were done for Savoy, especially "Parker's Mood" (on *Charlie Parker Memorial*

Vol. 2) and "Ko Ko" (*The Charlie Parker Story*), the problem of where to start is easily solved by **The Dial Masters** double album. The work for the Dial label, specially founded to record him, includes four sessions and a rehearsal performance (**Diggin' Diz**, who makes his only appearance here) from Bird's spell in Los Angeles during 1946 and 1947 and three sessions by his famous 1947 New York quintet with Davis, Jordan, Potter and Roach, augmented on the last occasion by trombonist Johnson.

The eighteen items of the latter group occupying the second CD are consistently excellent, but the mixed personnels of the earlier repertoire do not disguise Parker's superior invention. Examples are his stunning entrance on **A Night In Tunisia**, his jousting with the more swing-oriented Erroll Garner on **Hot Blues** and **Cool Blues** (the same tune at different tempos) and sympathetic accompaniment of the two vocals by Earl Coleman, and his comparatively light-hearted playing on **Relaxing At Camarillo**. The four tracks salvaged from his notorious pre-breakdown session (**Lover Man**, etc) show him barely coping, and throw everything else into relief.

There is much laudable playing from Thompson and Gray, and both the nineteen- and twenty-one-year-old editions of Miles are thinking on their feet. Max Roach, heard only at the New York sessions, is discreetly interactive and contributes a very occasional foretaste of Latin-jazz. But Parker is out front in all senses, whether on the super-fast **Klact-oveeseeds-tene** and **The Hymn** or the medium-tempo **Scrapple From The Apple** or the melodious yet thought-provoking ballads. Though it's often forgotten, Bird's ensemble themes, such as the last-named or **Quasimodo** or the blues **Bird Feathers**, have their own beauty.

While multiple versions of most of these pieces were released – and are available in more comprehensive reissues – focusing on the original singles presents an amazing concentration of unbeatable classics. It's a pity that the most celebrated performance of "Embraceable You" (initially thought too long for a single) is not here, but the subtly different B-take is equally impressive.

⮑We almost chose **Charlie Parker Memorial Vol. 2**,

Savoy, 1991 [1945–48]

74

Charlie Parker

Jazz At Massey Hall

OJC, 1989 (rec. 1953)

Parker (alto-sax), Dizzy Gillespie (trumpet), Bud Powell (piano), Charles Mingus (bass), Max Roach (drums).

Parker's short career barely lasted long enough for him to see the beginning (around 1954) of an age in which album releases could achieve the impact that single tracks had, back in the days of wind-up phonographs and juke-boxes. It's true that his affiliation from 1949 onwards with Norman Granz's labels (later rechristened Verve) led to groups of pieces with a guiding concept being recorded and released together – both on 78rpm singles and 10" LP – but their reissue on 12" LPs turned out to be posthumous. The only Parker album to make an impact during his lifetime was **Jazz At Massey Hall**, which was recorded outside his Granz contract and on which he appeared (via the pseudonym "Charlie Chan") as a member of "The Quintet Of The Year".

The year was 1953 and, because of the album's excellent music, the story behind it bears retelling. Toronto's "New Jazz Society" – in other words, fans opposed to the "old" jazz that seemed to have been superseded assembled an all-star group for their concert in Massey Hall, which has subsequently been seen as a last hurrah for pure bebop. Bird, Diz, Bud, Max and the recent arrival from Los Angeles, Mingus, were all experiencing hard times economically, but the fact that Mingus and Roach taped the gig and released it on their musician-owned Debut label gave it iconic status, and incidentally helped to revive interest in the classic bop style.

The hard times, and indeed the fact that the hall was only one third full, were soon forgotten as – with no rehearsal – the five performers launched into a reunion to end all reunions. (The concert also contained a set by a Canadian big band, an unaccompanied drum feature for Max Roach and twenty minutes of the Bud Powell Trio – the last two were issued separately by Debut.) The repertoire consisted of a rerun of old favourites, all of them written ten or more years earlier at the dawn of the bop era. By far the best known in the long term is Gillespie's **A Night In Tunisia**, which by this date had been recorded separately by its composer, by Parker and by Powell with Roach, but never together (bootlegs apart). Warhorses such as **Salt Peanuts** and Tadd Dameron's **Hot House** are joined by **Perdido**, a tune from the Ellington book that pointed the way for boppers, and by one of their preferred standards, **All The Things You Are**.

Differences between the soloists' work and their classic studio versions of some of the same material reflect their approach to live performance. Gillespie seems most aware of the audience, not only amusing them with the occasional musical quotation or bit of visual business but sometimes choosing his high notes for their dazzlement; yet his solos show exemplary construction and are superior to most of his other contemporary recordings. Parker also plays with a certain levity at times, but his passion and precision are unmistakable, while Powell weaves a hallucinatory accompaniment on "Things" and spins some fine solos, especially on "Hot House". The latter has one of only two spots by Mingus, while Roach – heard more prominently than on much of his early studio work – drives the whole exciting show with magisterial authority.

The balance on the horns is somewhat variable, but no one has ever stopped listening to the music long enough to complain about the sound. Though Mingus remedied the relative inaudibility of his bass by overdubbing everything except his solos, this too has never detracted from one of the most live recordings in all jazz.

⮑We almost chose **Bird And Fats Live At Birdland**,

Cool & Blue, 1992 [1950]

75

Art Pepper

Art Pepper Meets The Rhythm Section

OJC, 1988 (rec. 1957)

Pepper (alto-sax), Red Garland (piano), Paul Chambers (bass), Philly Joe Jones (drums).

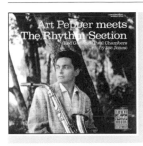

Pepper came to prominence in the Stan Kenton band of the late 1940s and, like all the altoists of his generation, was awestruck by the seemingly supernatural ability of Charlie Parker. However, he soon came up with a different slant, perhaps because before Kenton he'd worked with an older alto master, Benny Carter, and was nurtured in the nightlife of Los Angeles's black entertainment centre, Central Avenue. Here, contemporary jazz mingled with popular music on a non-discriminatory basis and the area's alumni, such as Dexter Gordon and Charles Mingus, were often to be found playing more basic swing and blues.

Art's style was touched by the phrasing of Lester Young as well as the energy of Parker, and his compromise solution soon became the accepted West Coast alto approach during the 1950s. Sadly, Pepper was also impressed by Bird's legendary appetite for hard drugs and – like so many young musicians coming to what should have been maturity – followed his example. Unfortunately Art didn't handle the experience so well, being unable to avoid repeated arrests and spending a large part of his life confined by the authorities. This not only underlined some aspects of his personality that came to the fore in his later music but, following the publication of a brutally revealing autobiography in 1979, gave him a charismatic notoriety and (briefly) the career to go with it.

Art Pepper Meets The Rhythm Section is one of the very best albums from the first half of his life, though run a close second by *The Art Of Pepper* recorded a couple of months later. Part of the reason for its success is undoubtedly its total lack of preparation and consequent jam-session-like spontaneity. (In the autobiography, ironically titled *Straight Life* after one of the tunes here, Pepper claims his wife had accepted the booking without notifying him until the day of recording but, characteristically, he exaggerated the pressure on him by insisting he hadn't played for six months – despite appearing on at least fourteen albums during that period.) Many jazz dates made during the 1950s, not only on the West Coast, undermined their intended formality by too much preparation and, while the opposite situation can create uninteresting results, it triumphantly brings out the latent qualities in an emotive player like Pepper.

His unfamiliarity with the rest of the quartet, except by reputation, is relieved by their familiarity with each other. Garland, Chambers and Jones were *the* rhythm-section of the day, not merely because they worked for *the* group (Miles Davis's quintet with John Coltrane) but because of their poised combination of weightlessness and drive – the duo of Chambers and Jones in particular being so dynamic that they appeared on countless other albums. In this post-Lester setting, which contrasts with most of their work elsewhere, they support Pepper to the hilt without overpowering him and fit with a will into such uncharacteristic material as Art's Dixieland choice, **Jazz Me Blues**, and even a swing waltz.

According to Pepper, they also suggested a couple of tunes that turn out to be eminently suitable for him, the bouncy **You'd Be So Nice To Come Home To** and the ballad **Imagination**. Resisting the thought that such cooperation across racial lines (still relatively unusual at the time) was only possible because the trio were all addicts too, it's reasonable to conclude that this is one 1950s West Coast session that has stood the test of time.

⮫We almost chose **The Art Of Pepper**, Blue Note, 1988 [1957]

76

Oscar Peterson

Oscar Peterson Trio + One

Verve, 1998 (rec. 1964)

Peterson (piano), Clark Terry (trumpet, flugelhorn, vocals), Ray Brown (bass), Ed Thigpen (drums).

Peterson's affable personality is one of the major factors in making him the most popular pianist of the last half-century — that and his amazing technical facility and his propensity to swing at the drop of a hat. But his musical qualities could easily count for little when seated at the keyboard (compared to instrumentalists who stand behind a microphone) if what he played didn't also communicate to the listener.

Although he has succeeded in continually expanding his all-conquering ability, nevertheless — like many other pianists such as Art Tatum, Erroll Garner and his idol Nat King Cole (in his days as a player) — Peterson's formative period as a sideman was brief and his star appeared in the firmament virtually overnight. The effect was particularly dramatic in Oscar's case because the early years took place in Montreal, Canada, and the pretended informality of his 1949 American debut — because of the absence of a work permit — was contradicted by its taking place during a concert at Carnegie Hall. Under the aegis of manager-promoter Norman Granz, Peterson spent much of the 1950s expanding his ensemble experience by leading his new American trio, by backing Jazz At The Philharmonic's touring jam sessions and working on albums with everyone who appeared on the Clef and Verve labels.

As a result, he was the most prolific recording artist of the period (for a while setting a standard of frequency barely matched by such as David Murray), and the fact that all of his output was for one producer in no way dented his listeners' or his own enthusiasm. His long 1950s series of single-composer albums preceded those of Ella Fitzgerald (or anyone else), while his accompaniments for Ella, Louis, Billie, Anita O'Day and a host of instrumentalists form a remarkably consistent body of work. Only after Granz sold Verve did Oscar work with other producers and eventually with other labels such as Mercury, for whom his debut (now reissued, confusingly, under the Verve imprint) was **Oscar Peterson Trio + One**.

This time the choice of front-line artist was Peterson's rather than a producer's and, though a younger musician than most of Granz's stable, a swing-oriented player of Oscar's own generation. Ex-Ellingtonian trumpeter Terry was just beginning to be recognized as a unique stylist who drew on influences as diverse as Rex Stewart, Charlie Shavers and Dizzy Gillespie, and his impish humour comes through clearly despite considerable technical virtuosity. His use of growls, bent notes and various mutes is illustrated throughout, while his lyricism surfaces on Peterson's **Roundalay** and the ballad **Jim**, the track which features his party trick of playing alternate phrases on trumpet and flugelhorn (holding one in each hand). His other party trick of imitating old-time blues singers in a type of wordless, consonant-less scat adds two brief highlights to the album, the uptempo **Mumbles** and a hilarious conversation between "male" and "female" voices.

The versatile, well-oiled trio – in which Ray Brown had partnered the pianist for nearly fifteen years and Thigpen a mere five – often steal the show with their intensely rhythmic momentum, even at slow tempo. Peterson's own playing is seen from all its best angles, including the dancing lines of a bouncy **Mack The Knife**, the occasional Tatum allusions in **I Want A Little Girl** and the sombre harmonies of **They Didn't Believe Me**. Certainly, the combination of Clark and Oscar comes off well, but this is also an excellent achievement for Peterson's trio.

⮌We almost chose **The Jazz Soul Of Oscar Peterson**,

Verve, 1996 [1959–62]

77

Bud Powell

The Amazing Bud Powell Vol. 1

Blue Note, 1995 (rec. 1949–51)

Powell (piano), Fats Navarro (trumpet), Sonny Rollins (tenor-sax), Tommy Potter, Curly Russell (bass), Roy Haynes, Max Roach (drums).

The enormous contribution to jazz piano of Bud Powell is still, at the time of writing, downgraded or ignored by the majority of listeners. His image and reputation have not been helped by factors such as the stigma of mental illness and – possibly not unconnected – his aloofness from fellow musicians with the exception of a very few close colleagues. Yet it says something that Horace Silver, Bill Evans, Herbie Hancock, Chick Corea, Keith Jarrett, McCoy Tyner and Cecil Taylor all pay tribute to Powell, while Corea and Jarrett among many others have covered his compositions.

Most jazz pianists before him were either virtuoso solo performers, who sounded unnaturally confined within a rhythm-section (Art Tatum is merely the most extreme example), or, in a few cases, committed rhythm-section players who seemed uncomfortable when given solo space. Powell raised the stakes for the latter – at the same period as Charlie Christian did for guitarists and Jimmie Blanton for double bassists – by giving them a new role that combined driving rhythm work with the ability to solo as intensely and communicatively as horn-players. The fact that this innovation occurred at the start of the bop era was no coincidence and, were it not for Powell's contribution, the piano could have become sidelined in bebop just as easily as was the clarinet.

Instead, he was seen early on as a natural counterpart of Parker and Gillespie, not only talking their language but sometimes sounding more commanding and fluent than they were. His 1940s recording sessions backing Dexter Gordon, Sonny Stitt, J.J. Johnson and, on one memorable occasion, Parker and Miles Davis, show the pianist perfectly capable of stealing their thunder with his incisive ideas and percussive tone. Though far from his best on the famous *Jazz At Massey Hall* album discussed under Parker, he not only holds his own but is consistently inventive, in a way that he found harder to achieve as his life became more problematic.

The years 1949–51 were, relatively speaking, a state of grace for Powell and this album presents two high spots of his career. He was already to be heard (like many pianists both before and after) leading groups without horn players, in public and in the studio, but the 1949 session has the advantage for new listeners of placing him in a typical bop quintet setting. Indeed, these eight tracks may be said to anticipate the hard-bop of the late 1950s, with their catchy themes punched out by Gillespie's rival, trumpeter Fats Navarro, and the teenage Sonny Rollins on one of his earliest recordings. The forceful rhythm-section of Potter and Haynes stimulates the soloists, none more so than the composer, and his stamina on two versions of the uptempo **Wail** is breathtaking.

On the surface, the trio set with Russell and Roach (which is continued on a separately available *Vol. 2*) is more relaxed, but it's instructive to hear the pianist's comparatively sunny readings of the Parker theme **Ornithology** and his individual approach to **Over The Rainbow**. The standout here, however, is the mambo-jazz of **Un Poco Loco**, in which Roach's hypnotic cowbell beat challenges Powell to quite different solos on three separate takes. The fact that several pieces on the album are included in more than one version should not deter anyone from savouring the improvisations from all concerned and, certainly, there can never be enough Powell from this period.

⮑We almost chose **The Ultimate Bud Powell**, Verve, 1998 [1949–56]

78

Joshua Redman

Wish

Warner, 1993

Redman (tenor sax), Pat Metheny (guitar), Charlie Haden (bass), Billy Higgins (drums).

Not many jazz fans had heard of Joshua Redman when he won the Thelonious Monk Competition's saxophone prize in 1991 – the son of well-known saxophonist Dewey Redman, he was apparently set on a career in law. That changed dramatically, because he soon signed for a major label, sold plenty of albums and was warmly received wherever he appeared. Sideman jobs, including a stint with Paul Motian's Electric Bebop Band, were relatively few, as demand grew for him to be the person in charge.

Just 24 when **Wish** was recorded, he shows a maturity that seems barely credible given his experience to date, and more than justifies any hype going. Whether or not he is the best saxophone player of his generation, whatever that may mean, he certainly proves himself capable of grabbing attention in a programme that pits him alongside three very distinguished musicians and where, being the only horn, he often has to carry theme-statements and make them count. This he does to maximum effect on **Make Sure You're Sure** by Stevie Wonder, on **We Had A Sister** by Pat Metheny, on the title tune (a kind of rockaballad of his own) and, most commendably, on Eric Clapton's **Tears In Heaven**, which he plays from beginning to end with Metheny's acoustic guitar as the only support. By any yardstick, that is classy stuff.

Redman's significance rests in part on a simple matter of accessibility. The combined influence of John Coltrane and several free blowers had conditioned hard-core fans to expect fast runs and/or freakish noises from their tenors. The prevailing tenor sound was harsh. Along comes a young man with an appealingly softish, pliable tone and the knack of building understandable sequences in which the stirring bits come where they make the greatest impact – Sonny Rollins inspired him, and he reminds one of Lester Young's belief that jazz solos should tell a story. His tunes are hummable and he gets through to a wider public without compromising the jazz, so the hard core also accept him.

The odd dissenter may complain about clocks being turned back but, in the Looking Glass arena where such debates take place, you cannot make that charge stick to anyone whose repertory includes songs by the likes of Eric Clapton. Nor, for that matter, the likes of Ornette Coleman, whose **Turnaround**, a favourite of Metheny's, is the opening track and draws from Redman a few hints of Coleman's intonation. Here, and on the quicker minor-keyed pieces – **The Deserving Many**, a romp the early Jazz Messengers might have tackled, and Metheny's blues, **Whittlin'** – Redman paces himself effortlessly, timing his trademark high-against-low-register contrasts to perfection. Charlie Parker's **Moose The Mooche**, another lively track, may be a programmatic device intended to attract any passing bebop trade; even if Redman does little new, he builds the solo with his usual assurance.

For a specific period this was a working quartet, and the final tracks gain presence and impact from being recorded live at the Village Vanguard. Metheny reserves his strongest efforts on these, stroking octaves for a while after Redman states the theme on **Wish** and switching between single lines and chords on **Blues For Pat**, which Charlie Haden dedicated to him some years ago. Haden himself takes a typical solo, squeezing the most from a few notes during a superbly evocative conclusion before Redman eases in to prove he can hold his own with heavyweights on their own ground.

⮑We almost chose **Beyond**, Warner, 2000

79

Django Reinhardt/Stéphane Grappelli

The Quintessential Django Reinhardt & Stéphane Grappelli

ΛƐV Living Era, 1008

Reinhardt (guitar), Grappelli (violin), Hubert Rostaing, Alix Combelle (clarinet), Joseph Reinhardt, Roger Chaput, Pierre "Baro" Ferret, Marcel Bianchi, Eugene Vees (guitar), Louis Vola, Tony Rovira, Emmanuel Soudieux (bass), Pierre Fuoad (drums), Freddie Taylor (vocals).

"Europe's pre-eminent jazz instrumentalist of all time!" is how Duke Ellington described Belgian guitarist Django Reinhardt, whose emergence onto the international jazz scene in the 1930s (with a Parisian-based group) came from left field, in the face of America's audible artistic supremacy.

Reinhardt has regularly been labelled a "genius" and in his case the label is justified. Born in Liverchies near Charleroi in 1910, he began playing a banjo guitar at the age of twelve and after grievous injuries in a caravan fire in 1928 re-perfected his fingerboard technique using (principally) two fingers only of his left hand. By 1934, in Paris, the handsome young gypsy had been featured in concerts for the "Hot Club de France" and met with Stéphane Grappelli, a trained pianist who by this time was playing violin with the touring group Gregor and his Gregorians. Together they agreed to form a quintet and after a debut in December 1934 at the Ecole Normale appeared on February 23, 1935 in concert at the Salle Pleyel, Paris, with American tenorist Coleman Hawkins. From then on, recording for Ultraphone, Decca and later HMV, the "Quintet of the Hot Club of France" became internationally famous, touring throughout Europe (including England and the London Palladium in 1938) and remaining together despite internal tensions until the war, by which time they had produced a classic discography of over two hundred sides. Reinhardt, ever the musical wanderer, died in 1953; Grappelli survived him by over forty years emerging in 1972 for a triumphant international renaissance.

Ray Crick's elegantly presented compilation is a connoisseur's delight, concentrating solely on the output of this super-influential group whose formats and music have been regularly recreated ever since. Crick's selections escort us through many of the Quintet's greatest moments, encompassing their output for Ultraphone, Decca and HMV and illustrating the tailored perfection of the group as well as the inspiration which regularly, at this period, calls the listener's ear back to the guitar of Reinhardt. There are endless high spots, starting at track one with **Dinah**, a tune that Reinhardt and Grappelli enjoyed playing together while they were working with bassist Louis Vola's orchestra at the Hotel Claridge in 1934; Reinhardt effortlessly changes key twice within one chorus. On **I'm Confessin'** his solo is an effortless *tour de force* and **I've Had My Moments**, which starts slow then accelerates to full power, has his lightning excursions into chordal atonality – a device he uses again on **Limehouse Blues**. After Grappelli's effectively vibrato-free opening chorus and solo here, Reinhardt's superlative solo includes a striking opening set of descending semi-tone clusters amid three choruses of simply extraordinary improvisation which sets skipping single lines against dramatic chorded figures. The guitarist constantly grabs your attention (Grappelli's peak years were to come later) and his **Improvisation** (track seventeen) is possibly the greatest jazz guitar solo on record, though his trio version of **I'll See You In My Dreams** runs it close. Spread through the collection are many more classics, among them **Swing Guitars**, the jaunty **Daphne**, **Minor Swing**, **Sweet Georgia Brown** and **Nuages**. This is a definitive collection, but listeners should look out too for more similarly indispensable Reinhardt sides recorded with American friends including Bill Coleman, Dickie Wells, Coleman Hawkins and Benny Carter.

⮐We almost chose **Django & His American Friends**,

DRG, 1998, 3-CDs [1935–45]

80

Max Roach

We Insist! – Freedom Now Suite

Candid, 1988 (rec. 1960)

Roach (drums), Booker Little (trumpet), Julian Priester (trombone), Walter Benton, Coleman Hawkins (tenor-sax), James Schenck (bass), Michael Olatunji, Ray Mantillo, Thomas DuVall (percussion), Abbey Lincoln (vocals).

Roach's importance in completing the rhythmic revolution of the bebop era is hardly likely to be underestimated at this stage. The fact that he appears on superior albums by Charlie Parker and Bud Powell speaks for itself, and hearing how he discovered the language necessary to complement their innovations is a joy to this day. But, whereas the foreshortened careers of both altoist and pianist prevented continued development of their early work, Roach on the other hand became an open-minded adventurer for the next half-century.

His 1954–56 quintet with Clifford Brown (see p.27) laid some of the foundations for both "hard-bop" and "modal jazz" while, after Brownie's tragic death, Roach went on to explore pianoless groups, odd-numbered time signatures and extended improvisation with his ex-sideman Sonny Rollins. In addition he expanded his percussive sensitivity, while a previously dormant compositional talent emerged with arrangements and original themes for three-piece front line (trumpet, tenor and trombone or tuba) that predated the use of such a line-up in Art Blakey's groups by several years. During this period, he also found a promising trumpet partner (soon to die even younger than Brown) in Booker Little, who was much more of a conscious modernist than his famous predecessor.

Despite the obvious seriousness of purpose in Roach's music of the late 1950s, few listeners were prepared for what he achieved with this 1960 album. Impelled by the civil rights movement, and in particular the lunch-counter sit-ins depicted on the cover, the drummer created a suite discussing different aspects of the racial situation in the US. Not entirely without precedent (Duke Ellington's 1943 *Black, Brown And Beige* dealt with similar subject matter), Roach didn't restrict himself to historical depiction but issued a call to further action. Thanks to the vocal contribution of his then-partner Abbey Lincoln and the lyrics of activist-songwriter Oscar Brown Jr, **We Insist!** was a statement strong enough to provoke hostility in some observers and a new understanding in others.

Driva' Man combines a whole-tone blues in 5/4 time with the simplicity of a work-song, in which Roach's snare imitates the hammers or axes of slave labourers. Following this, the impulsive uptempo of **Freedom Day** takes its cue from the apparent (and delusive) emancipation proclaimed at the end of the American Civil War. The centrepiece of the album is the **Triptych**, featuring only the menacing drums of the leader and the wordless voice of Lincoln, who traverses the journey from sorrowful resignation to anger finally unleashed to exhausted self-confidence. This was already a considerable achievement, but the remaining two sections of the suite bring an African dimension with the added percussionists, **All Africa** being a celebration of the tribes from which the slaves were taken and **Tears For Johannesburg** (another blues in 5/4) commenting on the Sharpeville massacre earlier in 1960.

Roach as director and performer is pivotal to the album but two solos by Booker Little are highlights, as is the committed expressiveness of older statesman Coleman Hawkins (who gave Max his first studio sessions) on the opening track. In the immediate aftermath of this recording came significant albums by Little (*Out Front*) and Abbey Lincoln (*Straight Ahead*), while Roach's example inspired such political works as Charlie Haden's *Liberation Music Orchestra* (Impulse) and Mike Westbrook's *Marching Song* (Deram).

⮑ We almost chose **Lift Every Voice And Sing**, Koch, 1999 [1971]

81

Sonny Rollins

Way Out West

OJC, 1988 (rec. 1957)

Rollins (tenor-sax), Ray Brown (bass), Shelly Manne (drums).

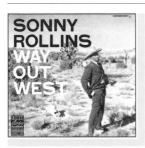

The great tenor saxophonist was born in New York City and grew up to idolize the popular Louis Jordan, before discovering that the legendary Coleman Hawkins was a near neighbour. Both Hawk and Lester Young, along with the much younger Dexter Gordon, were admired and understood by Rollins but the influence that all of his own generation initially had to meet head-on was that of Charlie Parker who, Rollins says, allowed him "to glimpse the possibilities of unfettered improvisation".

The key factor that distinguishes Sonny from most of his contemporaries outside the "free-jazz" area is the amount of store he sets by improvisation. While bebop and later players usually abandoned a given melody in favour of variations as soon as possible, they were far from embarrassed about repeating some elements of these variations from night to night, or from tune to tune. By contrast, Rollins has an in-built melodic sense in his own variations – while, in addition, referring back more frequently to the original material – and yet constantly refuses to coast. Living on the creative edge has often been a source of frustration for him (he is seldom satisfied with a performance) and sometimes also for listeners, since (on a bad night) he avoids the easy solution of covering a lack of inspiration with formulaic filler.

However, his gargantuan energy, his enormous stamina, plus his rhythmic, harmonic and tonal resourcefulness quickly won over those critics who had accused him of unevenness in his early work with Powell (*The Amazing Bud Powell Vol. 1*), Davis (*Miles Davis And the Modern Jazz Giants*) and Monk (*Thelonious Monk/Sonny Rollins*). Between joining the Max Roach–Clifford Brown group in late 1955 and becoming a working bandleader two years later, he was in a state of grace that happened to coincide with the initial boom in long-playing records. Documented on a plethora of albums for several labels (from *Worktime* to *The Freedom Suite*), his invention was without peer and its appeal was only modified by the changing cast of sidemen.

Way Out West is therefore hardly more essential than any other item from this period. It is distinguished, however, by a number of factors – it put him together with unaccustomed colleagues, and it was the first time he had recorded without a pianist or guitarist, which he then did with considerable frequency. Making the absence of any chord instrument a virtue (as Ornette Coleman was about to do), Sonny's acute harmonic sense is obviously highlighted in such spare surroundings. The same strategy also liberated his rhythmic virtuosity to dialogue with the versatile Shelly Manne, who outdoes himself on several occasions, and Rollins was also fortunate to call on the supremely solid Ray Brown, then working with Oscar Peterson.

Marking his first trip to the West Coast, he chose two tunes (**Wagon Wheels** and Johnny Mercer's sardonic **I'm An Old Cowhand**) that would be spectacularly inappropriate for any other saxist, but balances them with two magisterial 1930s ballads, while **Come, Gone** is an uptempo romp through the even older "After You've Gone". The album omits any nod towards his Caribbean calypso heritage (which first surfaced on the previous year's modestly titled *Saxophone Colossus*) but, while every other group of the day used four-bar exchanges to follow the main solos, Sonny's title tune here divides a couple of choruses into "fives". Generally showing why (along with Miles, Monk and Roach) he was one of the established musicians encouraging greater freedom in the music, *Way Out West* needs no such historical justification to be thoroughly enjoyable.

⮌We almost chose **Saxophone Colossus**, OJC, 1998 [1956]

82

Alex von Schlippenbach

Elf Bagatellen

FMP, 1990

Schlippenbach (piano), Evan Parker (soprano-sax, tenor-sax), Paul Lovens (drums).

Because it stresses the contingency of live performance and places a premium on artistic process rather than product, free improvisation is in some aspects antithetical to the notion of the "essential CD". Records are just dog-ears in an ongoing, always unfinished novel. But that philosophy hasn't mandated mediocre records, and there is at least a handful of indispensable documents of free music. With three of the strongest individual voices in improvised music from Europe, the Schlippenbach Trio operates at the pinnacle of collective improvisation.

A muscular session with moments of great sensitivity and playful interaction, **Elf Bagatellen** is their masterpiece. It's a beautiful recording, waxed in 1990 for Berlin's Free Music Production (FMP) label, and it bears testament both to the underlying connection of one wing of the European free scene to the jazz continuum, and to the personal vision of the best of its players. The music is totally improvised – no arrangements, no heads, no pre-ordained forms, no changes and no set strings of solos. But it is also highly structured, exquisitely detailed, with an organic sense of flow and an in-built logic that comes out of careful listening to each other, decisive action and interaction. Where other CDs by the trio – like the hard-hitting concert recording *Physics* (FMP) – offer long episodic tracks, this studio date is broken into a suite of shorter cuts. It's an ideal introduction to the joys of freely improvised music.

Some of the CD's brilliance comes from the fact that these musicians have worked together regularly since 1970, both as a trio and sometimes adding a bassist. Together, they've developed the kind of group identity that allows for the deepest free play. Evan Parker, arguably the single most advanced saxophonist since John Coltrane, arrived on the British jazz scene in the mid-1960s. On this outing Parker plays a short, stunning tenor solo (**K.K. Maximus**), and one can immediately hear how he has created a unique vocabulary out of special techniques, such as circular breathing, special tonguing devices, multiphonics and split tones, and a staggering digital dexterity. But it's his unparalleled sense of focus and his utterly musical application of that big trick-bag that make Parker the master.

The patriarch of German free piano, Schlippenbach burst forth slightly earlier in the 1960s, playing music deeply influenced by Horace Silver and Thelonious Monk. Soon involved exclusively in the world of free improvisation, he formed the seminal European free-music big group, Globe Unity Orchestra, and on the other end of the size spectrum he's released a number of great solo and duo records. Here he offers two brief solo studies (**Aries** and **Fux**) to book-end the date. He's a fiery, powerful, sometimes brutal musician, not afraid of direct jazz references (**Resurrection Of Yarak**), but clearly steeped in the classical piano repertoire. When Schlippenbach enters the immense world of German percussionist Paul Lovens – one of the most original musicians of our era, a genius timbre-manipulator and always a potential powderkeg – he often creates high-impact energy music: the palpable connection to American free jazz.

But there's plenty here indigenous to the pan-European scene: chamber-like restraint and elegance (**Bovist**), sheer sound exploration (**Elster-Werda Nocturno**), and Schlippenbach's brooding, late-romantic chords. Listen to the way Lovens and Parker square off at the end of **Sun-Luck: Revisited** – quick rolls on muted drums, splinters of sax shooting like sparks off a blacksmith's anvil.

⟳We almost chose **Physics**, FMP, 1993 [1991]

83

John Scofield

Time On My Hands

Blue Note, 1990 (rec. 1989)

Scofield (guitar), Joe Lovano (tenor-sax), Charlie Haden (bass), Jack DeJohnette (drums).

Of those who took major roles in bands led by Miles Davis during the 1980s, John Scofield received the biggest uplift to his career as a result. Earlier gigs with Billy Cobham and Gary Burton had put his name on the map, especially among supporters of so-called jazz-fusion. He then capitalized on the wider acclaim gained alongside Davis by forming a quartet featuring tenor saxophonist Joe Lovano, himself on the brink of acquiring critical status and fans by the bucketful after years as a semi-cult figure.

Having grafted a country-bluesy twang to what had been the jazz norm of single-note phrases performed with a slightly muffled sound, Scofield went on to develop a more integrated style. The balance changes, but chords that rumble or bite, twangy tones and flowing lines co-exist throughout almost every solo, whereas guitarists of comparable talent in the same field are inclined to switch according to context and mood. Albums such as this also indicate a talent for catchy tunes (to which he sometimes gives amusingly punning titles) that make excellent bases for improvisation.

Apart from Lovano, **Time On My Hands** replaces Scofield's touring rhythm-section with the all-star team of Charlie Haden and Jack DeJohnette, perhaps a shop-window ploy on Blue Note's part but one that does the music absolutely no harm. Haden's firm sound provides the perfect anchor, leaving

DeJohnette free to track the soloists and trade blow for blow, as he does behind Scofield on **Flower Power** and **Farmacology** and behind Lovano on **So Sue Me**.

The range of captivating material, all compositions by the leader, adds to the appeal. As examples of updated jazz riffs, **Wabash III** hints at the swing era, while **Stranger To The Light**, where DeJohnette is given a free run, is more abstract. Scofield's tunes often evoke Ornette Coleman around this period, the blues "Farmacology" and the Latin-crossed-with-country "So Sue Me" making the point.

Most offer potent examples of the guitarist's mix 'n' match approach. The best include "Flower Power", a theme in triple time for just the trio, presented by Scofield with plenty of chordal shading before he leaps into a solo full of imaginative lines, offset by metallic top notes and an arsenal of sound effects. "Farmacology" abounds with pithy blues licks, and country-type whines predominate on "So Sue Me". On **Since You Asked**, an attractive slow-medium ballad, he meshes the melody into his improvisations. Slightly related to the latter, but obviously aimed at the disco market, **Fat Lip** rocks hard, with atmospheric guitar and heavy drumming.

Lovano's ability to coax beguilingly smooth tones from the high register comes through on the relaxed "Since You Asked" and **Nocturnal Mission**. The main soloist on the latter, he effortlessly picks the choicest notes from the chords, repeating the process on the more aggressive "Farmacology" as Scofield piles up organ-type riffs in the background. When things get freer, as on "Stranger To The Light", with out-of-tempo drum licks thundering at his elbow, Lovano builds craftily around references to the theme.

That number highlights the contrasting roles adopted by DeJohnette and Haden, whose bass patterns hold it together. His solos are few and spare but, as ever, absolutely to the point, the strings ringing out loud and long on **Time And Tide** and **Be Hear Now**.

➲We almost chose **Grace Under Pressure**, Blue Note, 1992 [1991]

Artie Shaw

Begin The Beguine

ASV Living Era, 1993 (rec. 1938–41)

Shaw (clarinet, leader), with his Orchestra and "Gramercy Five", plus Helen Forrest, Billie Holiday, Tony Pastor (vocals), "Hot Lips" Page (trumpet, vocals).

Whereas Benny Goodman might tactfully be dubbed the "absent-minded professor of jazz clarinet", Artie Shaw, his neck-and-neck rival through all the swing-happy years, was just the opposite – a passionate, charismatic and intellectual spokesman for, amongst many other things, jazz, the jazz life and the predicament of the popular performer. Whereas Goodman's 1939 autobiography *The Kingdom Of Swing* was co-written largely by a somewhat bewildered collaborator, Irving Kolodin, Shaw's – written in 1955 and called *The Trouble With Cinderella* – was three times its length and subtitled *An Outline Of Identity*. The only thing the two men shared was disdain for the gewgaws of popular fame. Goodman turned his angry stare or "ray" onto an audience delightedly clapping to one of his Carnegie Hall solos in 1938; Shaw similarly dismissed jitterbugs, the limits of their musical appreciation and the cell-like prison of musical repetition night by night. By 1953 he had given up playing completely, while Goodman confined himself to old glories and clarinet practice until he died.

Shaw's playing was different – and some say preferable – to Goodman's, too. Warmer, more architectural and motivic, his perfectly sculpted phrases rode the beat with total rhythmic control (as did Goodman's) but with more in the way of pronounced inflections and regular drama, particularly in the clarinet's extreme upper register, of which Shaw was a master. His musical output – while probably lacking the ultimate elegance of Goodman's small groups – was more varied than his rival's; regularly employing strings (in various configurations from quartet up), intriguing fellow soloists (including a parade of great trumpeters, amongst them Henry "Red" Allen, Roy Eldridge, "Hot Lips" Page, and Billy Butterfield) and a team of great arrangers who regularly produced striking creations.

This excellent single-CD collection collates much of Shaw's most well-known and effective work, including his eight-million-selling "gold discs". These comprise his adopted theme tune **Begin The Beguine** (arranged by Jerry Gray), **Nightmare** (another one-time signature tune), the classic **Back Bay Shuffle**, **Traffic Jam**, and swaying string-decorated **Frenesi**, **Dancing In The Dark**, **Stardust** (which, along with classic Butterfield, has a Shaw clarinet solo simply perfect in conception and execution) and **Summit Ridge Drive** by his wonderfully neat "Gramercy Five", featuring Butterfield and a much-underrated titan of jazz piano, Johnny Guarnieri, manning the harpsichord. Compiler Vic Bellerby has done us a favour by including the equally well-rated B-side to "Summit Ridge Drive" (the busily swinging **Special Delivery Stomp**) and there are more classics here, including **St James Infirmary** (a two-part feature for Hot Lips Page's sinuous vocal and gruff shouting trumpet), **Any Old Time** (a definitively joyous swing song which Shaw wrote for Billie Holiday, and which she sings exquisitely) and one track for another well-respected singer, Helen Forrest – Holiday's good friend – who shines alongside her leader on **Deep Purple**. Less well-known choices include **Rosalie** (with vocal by Tony Pastor), **Lady Be Good** (1939) and **April In Paris** (1940), but all are excellent representations of Shaw. Left to last is his own monumental **Concerto For Clarinet**, originally a double-sided 12" 78 – a format more usually reserved for classical music. As usual, this is a definitive ASV collection, including Vic Bellerby's informative sleevenotes, for which the only minor qualification possible is that – as regularly in this series – you must look hard in the crowded booklet and sleeve to find out everything about one track. Oh well!

⮑We almost chose **Big Band Bash**, Giants of Jazz, 1990 [1938–41]

85

Wayne Shorter

Speak No Evil

Blue Note, 1999 (rec. 1964)

Shorter (tenor-sax), Freddie Hubbard (trumpet), Herbie Hancock (piano), Ron Carter (bass), Elvin Jones (drums).

Sometimes the greatest of artistic inventions exert the most noxious influence. It may be a sincere form of flattery, but imitation in jazz is at best a phase, at worst an early death. Listen to the facsimiles of Coltrane's astounding saxophone playing in two subsequent generations of horn players – imitation vanquishes imagination. The same could be said of Wayne Shorter's influential compositions. If you're listening for a main source for the pseudo-sophisticated harmonies and impressionistic melodies of the most mundane of today's mainstream jazz tunes, Shorter's gorgeous writing may well be to blame.

Shorter spent five years leading up to 1964 – the year he began a spate of recordings as a leader for Blue Note and also the year he joined the classic Miles Davis Quintet – with Art Blakey's core hard-bop outfit, the Jazz Messengers. Shorter was already accomplished as a composer, but some of the pieces featured on his own and Davis's records would eventually be recognized jazz standards. **Speak No Evil** was the saxophonist's third Blue Note date, and he's accompanied by his cohorts in the Davis Quintet, Ron Carter on bass and Herbie Hancock on piano, as well as exceptionally versatile trumpeter Freddie Hubbard and John Coltrane Quartet drummer Elvin Jones.

In the record's sleevenotes, Shorter says: "I was thinking of misty landscapes with wildflowers and strange, dimly-seen shapes – the kind of places where folklore and legends are born ... things like witch-burnings, too." That hazy, mystico-magical imagery is translated into music through intriguingly voiced, often ambiguous harmonies. The hard-bop gleam is still there – these are polished, precise pieces, and the main theme to **Witch Hunt** relies on brassy flash and a jolt of adrenaline, adroitly provided by Hubbard. But Shorter was mining late-romantic classical music for inspiration, as well as the expected bop resources; his elegant waltz **Dance Cadaverous** (of which there is an extra alternate take on the CD reissue), for instance, specifically makes use of Jean Sibelius's "Valse Triste" and there are fingerprints of the French impressionists all over Hancock's chromatically dense chord choices on the lovely **Wild Flower**. The title cut is urbane – slick even – with an unusual structure and cool held notes over shifting support. (The only technical mis-step on the session, sparklingly recorded by the pioneering engineer Rudy Van Gelder, is the fade-out on this cut, a compositional cop-out, very nearly unique in the Blue Note canon at this time.)

It's unfair to look exclusively at *Speak No Evil* in terms of its writing. Shorter was a great saxophone synthesist, integrating stylistic traits of Trane and Sonny Rollins, as well as grappling with some of Ornette Coleman's elastic phrasing. The ballad **Infant Eyes**, a vehicle for his tender tenor, shows the continuity between Shorter's improvising and composing. Hubbard plays a bit like a straight hard-bop holdover in places, like his slurring, gutsy solo on **Fee-Fi-Fo-Fum**, but it's in keeping with the bluesy tone of the piece and Shorter's turn is equally tough and gritty. Hancock's piano here and on his own acoustic outings as a leader set the agenda for a slew of saccharine tinklers who have little of his intelligence or personality. Jones, while not featured, is worth singling out for his astounding swing and adaptability – compare this with any of his contemporaneous recordings with Coltrane to see how he plays to the session at hand but maintains his individual style.

⮌We almost chose **Juju**, Blue Note, 1999 [1964]

86

Horace Silver

Blowin' The Blues Away

Blue Note, 1999 (rec. 1959)

Silver (piano), Blue Mitchell (trumpet), Junior Cook (tenor-sax), Gene Taylor (bass), Louis Hayes (drums).

Horace Silver was probably the most influential pianist of the 1950s, and certainly one of the most enjoyable of any period. His ascendancy began during the absence from the scene of Bud Powell and the initial incomprehension that greeted Thelonious Monk. By no coincidence, Silver combined the dynamism of the former with the latter's terseness, and added a bluesy phraseology reflecting his early interest in boogie-woogie and r&b. In addition, listeners weaned on these latter styles recognized Horace's gift for writing the kind of catchy tunes that made for hit records.

This was immediately discernible when he joined Stan Getz's group in the early 1950s, and was rapidly capitalized on in the first albums under his own name and with Art Blakey. Forming his quintet in 1956, he enjoyed a remarkable run of success with tracks such as "Senor Blues", "No Smokin'", "Filthy McNasty", "The Tokyo Blues", "Song For My Father", and on and on. While the last-named has been credited with inspiring all manner of artists including Steely Dan, the influence was also going in the opposite direction – in fact, more than Herbie Hancock's "Watermelon Man" or Lee Morgan's "The Sidewinder", "Song For My Father" sanctified the absorption of diluted Latin rhythms from soul music and established a kind of pre-fusion jazz catering to black audiences in the later 1960s (and revived two decades later as "acid-jazz"). Its popularity has therefore tended to obscure Silver's giant achievements when working within the swing-oriented rhythms of his earlier bands.

An essential example of this, **Blowin' The Blues Away**, also contains no fewer than three classic tunes. The title track is an uptempo blues with a choppy riff whose timing and shape is varied on each repeat (a little like Monk's "Straight, No Chaser"), while Silver's solo deals in much simpler riffs, including an outrageous quotation. The glorious **Sister Sadie**, the album's fake-gospel song, is based on a riff that had been around at least twenty years, but echoes the swing era also in using written backing figures behind the tenor solo and a couple of choruses of new ensemble riffs before reprising the opening melody. Although many of Silver's ballad numbers have been recorded as piano trio features, **Peace** has a carefully worked-out arrangement for trumpet and tenor, and even at this slow tempo Horace's piano betrays the influence of Monk.

Silver's function within the rhythm-section is extraordinary too, for if the aim of his brand of hard-bop is to recreate the excitement of the big-band style, his uniquely pushy accompaniments simulate whole brass and reed sections – and often the bass-drum too. The role of Hayes and Taylor is merely to lay down the tempo in a suitably aggressive manner, and even Mitchell and Cook's contributions are just intended to fill their space appropriately, for all the world like most big-band soloists. Mitchell, near the start of his five-year stint with Silver, honours the memory of Clifford Brown and, even in his latter period of prolific session-work, seldom played better than this. Cook, a more average player whose career continued into the early 1990s, certainly holds his own against the competition.

It's unfortunate that Silver is sometimes seen as an essentially lightweight artist – having hit tunes is not good for the image of a "serious" jazz musician. But the depth of his awareness of tradition, and the heights of his invention, easily withstand the test of time.

⮑We almost chose **Song For My Father**, Blue Note, 1999 [1963–64]

87

Jimmy Smith

The Sermon!

Blue Note, 2000 (rec. 1957–58)

Smith (organ), Lee Morgan (trumpet), Lou Donaldson, George Coleman (alto-sax), Tina Brooks (tenor-sax), Kenny Burrell, Eddie McFadden (guitar), Art Blakey, Donald Bailey (drums).

Fats Waller was probably the first to make convincing jazz use of the electric organ, but it was popularized in the early 1950s by such as Milt Buckner (former pianist with Lionel Hampton), Wild Bill Davis (ditto with Louis Jordan) and Bill Doggett (who replaced Davis with Jordan). All three worked at the interface of jazz with r&b, for the organ became r&b's equivalent to the swing era's brass sections.

Smith, having played piano around his native Philadelphia, had no national profile before switching to organ, yet in 1955 word spread that he had a revolutionary approach. Instead of big-band "section work", he based himself on the single-note lines of pianists influenced by Bud Powell with an admixture of the bluesy phraseology recently popularized by Horace Silver and the piano work of Ray Charles. The effect of this change, combined with the power of electricity, and especially the cutting tone obtained by Smith's particular choice of registration, created an exciting innovative sound that bludgeoned listeners and musicians alike into submission. (John Coltrane, who worked with him briefly in Philadelphia, said, "I'd wake up in the middle of the night, man, hearing that organ ... screaming at me.")

Following the immediate sales success of his 1956 trio albums, Smith's career intersected for a while with a phenomenon of the current recording boom, whereby labels such as Savoy, Verve and

Prestige would put a bunch of musicians in the studio for a "blowing session" – in other words, expecting them to fill a 12" LP with lengthy jams and a minimum of preparation. It worked brilliantly on **The Sermon!**, for, while Smith threatened to dominate proceedings, he was an inspiring leader. Actually, this album represents parts of two sessions, with the earlier one featuring his regular trio plus two newcomers, saxophonist George Coleman (on his original instrument, the alto) and trumpeter Lee Morgan. Morgan is retained for the second session six months later, with tenorist Tina Brooks and guitarist Kenny Burrell (also relative newcomers) and Blue Note veterans Lou Donaldson and Art Blakey.

Throughout the three long tracks – slow-medium blues, fast-medium bebop and a ballad – Smith energizes the music and directs the traffic, while his solos reveal a variety of ideas not always found in his later work. The nineteen-year-old Morgan is consistently impressive, revealing his great fondness for Clifford Brown on the ballad **Flamingo**. The title track is the twenty-minute *pièce de résistance*, starting with Smith's simple blues riff and gradually building in intensity as the soloists succeed one another. Brooks, whose career never took off the way Blue Note hoped, takes an impassioned, vocalized solo that puts Morgan and Donaldson on their mettle, and everyone's commitment to the cause is underlined by the fact that the piece gradually speeds up from 74 to 88 beats per minute by the end.

Though he normally tours fronting just a trio, some listeners prefer the sound of Smith battling it out with big-band brass sections (often contributed by Oliver Nelson), and it's true this widened his audience, just as it did for Wes Montgomery. These two even recorded a couple of albums together, including tracks with the inevitable big band, but Smith's best soulmate on records (usually busy leading his own trio) was always Burrell. As well as tracks on the present album's companion set, *House Party*, available material with Jimmy and Kenny together includes two fine sets adding saxophonist Stanley Turrentine, *Midnight Special* and *Back At The Chicken Shack*.

⮑ We almost chose **Midnight Special**, Blue Note, 1988 [1960]

88

Muggsy Spanier

The Great 16! Muggsy Spanier's Ragtime Band

RCA Victor, 1993 (rec. 1939)

Spanier (cornet), with George Brunis (trombone), Rod Cless (clarinet), Ray McKinstry, Bernie Billings, Nick Caiazza (tenor-sax), George Zack, Joe Bushkin (piano), Bob Casey (guitar), Pat Pattison, Bob Casey (bass), Marty Greenberg, Don Carter, Al Sidell (drums).

As one of the youthful generation of trumpeters who sat at the feet of King Oliver and Louis Armstrong learning their craft in 1920s Chicago, none was more impressed by Oliver than the youthful Muggsy Spanier, who picked up central elements from Oliver (the elusive art of playing straight lead in an ensemble, plus cunning use of muted effects) and carried them forward into his own celebrity career. Spanier – who also loved Tommy Ladnier – was principally a mid-register player. But almost no one could drive a Dixieland band down with the infallible on-the-beat lead that he had mastered (leaving all the right gaps for his fellow front-liners to fill) and his fat, open tone was often capped with plunger or cup-mute, acquiring a unique turkey-gobble effect at note's end that Oliver would have loved.

From spring 1939 Spanier organized a new band for a highly successful residency at Chicago's Hotel Sherman which lasted for six months before a move to Nick's club in Greenwich Village, New York. In July 1939, Spanier cut the first of sixteen 78 rpm sides for RCA Victor's Bluebird label and soon it was plain that every title was to be a classic. By the time the last four were recorded in December, a series was complete which would become known as Spanier's **The Great 16!** and recognized as (possibly) the greatest Dixieland jazz on record. Around him Spanier organized a stylistically unified troupe including trombonist George Brunis and the hugely talented clarinettist, Rod Cless. Tenorists Ray McKinstry, Bernie Billings and Nick Caiazza successively filled the tenor chair and other minor changes occurred, including the replacement of a highly capable pianist, George Zack, for twelve of the sixteen titles, by the great Joe Bushkin. It was Bushkin who contributed the introduction to one of the *16's* classics, **Relaxin' At The Touro**, after which he was credited as co-composer.

"Touro" was the opening track on the original LP reissue; a profound blues on which Spanier's preaching cornet opening is reverently backed by choreographed long notes and a harmonized concluding downward phrase after twelve bars. This illustrates one of the wonders of these titles – their inspired ensemble choreography, even in what would appear to be ad lib situations. Some years ago RCA Bluebird issued a fascinating CD (see below) including alternative takes placed directly after the originals. These alternates, whose existence had long been questioned and which were virtually indistinguishable from the originals, demonstrated both the sophistication of this musical choreography and how gratifyingly it failed to affect the music's heat (no doubt the Spanier band's regular nightly residency at the Sherman helped these fine points to materialize on the stand). Every track, as history quickly acknowledged, is a classic, but (highly) selected high spots include **That Da Da Strain** (with tight ensemble and an inspired Cless), **I Wish I Could Shimmy Like My Sister Kate** (Brunis's fine vocal and a slam-bang ensemble break at the end) and the near-operatic band cadence which precedes a final reprise on **At Sundown**. Brunis sings wonderfully again on the lighter-than-air **Dinah** (graced with its verse, played by the leader out of tempo) and his reverend trombone interlude preceding Spanier's menacing plunger-mute finale to **Lonesome Road** is almost eerie. Throughout Cless (outstanding on **Eccentric**) is heroic, but really all is wonder here – the unity of talent, purpose and inspiration on these sides makes them brim with irresistible life, though all the old heroes are gone.

⟳We almost chose **Muggsy Spanier 1939: The "Ragtime Band" Sessions**, RCA Bluebird [1995].

89

Sun Ra And His Myth Science Arkestra

Fate In A Pleasant Mood/When Sun Comes Out

Evidence, 1993 (rec. 1960–63)

Ra (piano, electric-celeste, percussion), two groups including Phil Cohran, Walter Miller, Lucious Randolph (trumpet), Nate Pryor (trombone), Marshall Allen (alto-sax, flute), Danny Davis (alto-sax), John Gilmore (tenor-sax), Pat Patrick (baritone-sax, percussion), Ronnie Boykins (bass), Clifford Jarvis, Lex Humphries (drums), Theda Barbara (vocals).

Pianist, visionary and bandleader Sun Ra had a very special relationship to the idea of the record album. To the point: Robert Campbell and Chris Trent's recently released discography, *The Earthly Recordings Of Sun Ra* (Cadence Books) tips the scales at a heavyweight 847 pages, documenting well over 150 commercially released records under Ra's name and hundreds of studio sessions and recorded live concerts. What's remarkable in this is not only the volume and diversity of musical material – from doo-wop and r&b to bop to experimental electronic music to through-composed and fiercely open orchestral jazz – but also the flexible relationship Ra maintained with the business of recording. Ra released LPs on large labels like A&M and independents like Savoy, but he was, along with his business partner Alton Abraham, also the architect of the most grandiose artist-run record company in jazz history, Saturn Records.

For the non-specialist, the music of Saturn was all but impossible to hear until about ten years ago. Virtually undistributed in the era they were produced, the original records were normally sold from the stage by the band. A deal with ABC/Impulse! in the 1970s put a few reissued Saturns into wider circulation, but that agreement quickly went awry, and the music remained largely dormant until Evidence began licensing some of them for

CD reissue in 1991. Evidence has now released 21 CDs, some, like this one, compiling more than one LP.

To become absorbed in the Ra oeuvre is to start to fit together parts of an intricate historical and aesthetic puzzle, which makes prioritizing a single record difficult. The early period, when Ra was based in Chicago, includes a wide array of approaches to renovating the big band. There are flashes of Tadd Dameron, Mingus, Ellington, Martin Denny, even Liberace, in the flamboyant and exotic arrangements he constructed for his bands at the time. **Fate In A Pleasant Mood** (which was titled, on the spine of its first issue, *Faith In A Pleasant Mood*, exemplifying both Ra's interest in wordplay and the philosophical ideas that lay veiled in some of his work) comes from the end of the Chicago years, while **When Sun Comes Out** was recorded in rehearsals just after Ra relocated to New York in 1961, when the music was growing more experimental and expressionistic.

The Others In Their World, Lights On A Satellite and the showy **Ankhnaton** demonstrate what an ingenious composer Ra was, with subtle little melodic moves that bump the otherwise straight themes out of line; all three include great lead parts for featured trumpeter Phil Cohran. Marshall Allen's flute tunes, like **Space Mates**, are enough to win over even the most vehement flute-ophobe. But Ra's secret weapon was John Gilmore, one of the all-time greatest and – because he devoted most of his career to the Arkestra – most overlooked of tenor saxophonists; listen to his concise, rhythm-sensitive solo on the jagged **Distant Stars**, his more elaborate, looping venture on **The Rainmaker**, and his searching bass clarinet on **Dimensions In Time**.

The looser New York LP begins with an out-of-tempo, wordless vocal, **Circe**, that foreshadows the Afrocentric scat of innumerable 1970s groups. **We Travel The Spaceways** is a classic space-chant, **Brazilian Sun** rests on the perfect funky ostinato of bassist Ronnie Boykins, and **Calling Planet Earth** contains a volcanic baritone solo by Pat Patrick. Acquire this stellar disc and enter the custom-built labyrinth of Mr Ra, an absolute American original.

⮑We almost chose **Jazz In Silhouette**, Evidence, 1991 [1958]

90

John Surman

The Amazing Adventures Of Simon Simon

ECM, undated (rec. 1981)

Surman (soprano-sax, baritone-sax, bass-clarinet, synth), Jack DeJohnette (electric-piano, drums, congas).

Soon after arriving in London from his native Plymouth, John Surman was ranked among the brightest young stars of the 1960s jazz renaissance, and not just by locals. Then playing mostly the baritone saxophone, he extended the instrument's effective range. Later, he recaptured that pioneering spirit by blending folk forms with electronics, his *Westering Home* album (Island, 1972) creating a pastoral aura of the kind identified eventually and indelibly with the ECM label. Keeping up the technological pace, he supplemented overdubs by taking every advantage of synthesized sounds, sequencers, tape loops and the like once they hit the streets, regularly giving before audiences the one-man show that had become a staple on his albums.

An accomplished pianist on top of being one of the best drummers around, Jack DeJohnette has collaborated regularly with Surman. Compared to the shared input of more recent duets, this early meeting finds DeJohnette playing a subordinate role, and not simply because Surman wrote five of the nine pieces and arranged the traditional **Lady Margaret's Air**. Very much in the style of his solo albums since *Westering Home*, the cool, pellucid overlay is often challenged by disquiet creeping up from below, whether through the presence of percussion or through Surman's pre-programming. The titles and their order of appearance imply a narrative that depicts

Simon's adventures, though connections between hunting in Kent and the halls of a mythological sea god are tenuous enough for us not to bother overmuch and to treat the whole on its merits.

The longest track, **Nestor's Saga**, begins with the warm, throaty sound of the bass clarinet over static harmony produced by repetitive keyboard patterns. Suddenly, the patterns modulate and, as he follows each change, Surman introduces fresh ideas that expand the piece organically. Drums come in towards the close and set a fast tempo, by which time he has added the soprano saxophone, ready for a duet where each instrument takes turns to ride the cymbal beat. The brooding atmosphere is highlighted further on **Within The Halls Of Neptune**. Rumbles from the synthesizer – appropriately giving a nod to Grieg's "In The Hall Of The Mountain King" – underpin improvisation that shows Surman has lost none of his legendary command of the baritone, while extracting even more richness from the intrinsically gruff, furry sound. The baritone's range under Surman's fingers gets more of an airing on **Fide Et Amore** where, accompanied by DeJohnette's electric piano, the volume barely rises as he hits the highest notes.

A feeling for the dance dominates **Kentish Hunting** and **Merry Pranks**. On the former, a kind of jig in triple time, the soprano takes off over a baritone riff. Drums provide the beat on "Merry Pranks", another jig, that opens and closes with a bass-clarinet duet. DeJohnette comes to the fore on **Phoenix And The Fire**; one of the wholly improvised pieces, it starts with a light cymbal beat behind the soprano. As the drums grow more agitated, so Surman reacts by choking noise from the soprano and then, over DeJohnette's most elaborate drumming of the album, he leaps into a passage of circular breathing. The drums, plus a wind ensemble, appear on the closing piece, **A Fitting Epitaph**, another feature for Surman's burnished baritone sound that gives the suite its serene and stately conclusion.

⊃We almost chose **Stranger Than Fiction**, ECM, 1994 [1993]

91

Art Tatum

Art Tatum's Finest Hour

Verve, 2000 (rec. 1934–55)

Tatum (piano solos), with Joe Thomas (trumpet), Edmond Hall (clarinet), John Collins, Tiny Grimes (guitar), Billy Taylor, Slam Stewart (bass), Eddie Dougherty (drums), Joe Turner (vocals).

In the world of jazz, where free expression pervades, superlatives are looked on with suspicion. But for most informed jazz persons Art Tatum is still acknowledged as the greatest pianist of all. "Maybe this will explain Art," said Teddy Wilson, a respected friend and brilliant contemporary. "You get all the finest jazz pianists in the world and let them play in [his] presence. Then let Art Tatum play [and] everyone there will sound like an amateur!" Wilson found this out early on, when tenorist Coleman Hawkins (who enjoyed inviting Wilson to join him in seeking out local jazz heroes in order to best them in territorial jam sessions) arrived in Toledo, Ohio, heard Tatum and rang Wilson in his hotel room. "Don't come," said Hawkins briefly, and put the phone down.

Tatum was unquestionably a genius on piano – his playing incorporated technical devices which have yet to be surpassed (or even explained) – but it was never technique alone that distinguished his performance. Misinformed critics who dismiss his work for its regular multi-note complexity miss its content, too; like Duke Ellington's, Tatum's work rewards repeated listening. His playing from the start was admired and sought out not only by the great classical pianist Vladimir Horowitz, but by talents from George Gershwin to Rachmaninoff, and nothing, it appears, has changed with the 21 century in jazz. André Previn –

a performer who spans both the jazz and classical camps with distinction – confirms: "Any discussion as to the merits of pianists must start with his name and then, after a respectful pause, arguments are in order as to the *next* best in line. Art Tatum always has been, and always will be, the greatest!"

What is more mystifying is how he acquired his gifts. Duke Ellington reveals that, early on, "quite a lot of what Tatum was doing was taken right off the player-piano rolls!" (Ellington learned the same way), and this may help to explain both why Tatum was fond of piano set pieces, and for much of his career was best heard in solo or trio format. Despite odd meetings with compatible partners, including Benny Carter, Ben Webster and the fleet Buddy de Franco recorded for Norman Granz in the 1950s, his definition of "accompaniment" was frequently too florid for front-line partners, producing the effect of two people talking at once. This CD has just one self-led Tatum band track, **Wee Baby Blues** (delicately backing Joe Turner, whose performer weight keeps him in the foreground), and one by his scintillating trio with Tiny Grimes and Slam Stewart (**I Got Rhythm**, 1944) which leaves the listener wanting more. Probably, though, Tatum is best heard solo and this set collates nine of his acknowledged classics, including **Liza** (1934, in which, typically, he toys with the melody before attacking it at full pelt), **Tea For Two** (from 1939, in which he takes Youman's sequence up in fleet half-tones bar by bar), the fantastical **Tiger Rag** (from 1940) and a harmelodic masterpiece **Begin The Beguine**, from the same year. Later in the collection come six tracks from titles recorded in 1950 and 1955 at the home of Ray Heindorf (distinguished trumpeter-conductor and musical director for Twentieth Century Fox) during a party to celebrate the completion of a movie. The sound is practically state of the art and Tatum stretches out on solos including **Too Marvellous For Words**, which critic Martin Williams credits as "very likely the greatest single Tatum performance we are fortunate to have". Aptly titled, too.

⮑We almost chose **The Art Of Tatum: 25 Greatest Solo Performances**, ASV, 1995 [1932–44]

92

Cecil Taylor

Silent Tongues

Freedom, 1992 (rec. 1974)

Taylor (piano).

In a variety of small-group contexts, pianist Cecil Taylor emerged in the mid-1950s, challenging and expanding the basic precepts of jazz harmony and its conventional relationship to form. Taylor's use of clusters and abrupt, violent rhythms, which sometimes erupted out of an unsuspecting ballad, were taken as an affront by some listeners, a radical call to arms by others. He's now treated as something of a pariah by neo-conservatives like Stanley Crouch (once a booster of Taylor's) and Wynton Marsalis, who claim that he falls far afield of jazz altogether and that because he studied Olivier Messiaen he should be classified as avant-garde classical. Funny that nobody ever made the same claim about Ellington or Bird for having checked into Stravinsky.

Taylor, however, needs no pundits to justify or categorize his music. Since the late 1960s, he has also been creating an utterly unique approach to unaccompanied piano. Unfettered by other musicians, Taylor can sculpt an hour-long solo like nobody's business; to do so, he's created a language that's so highly personalized that hearing him alone is arguably the only way to have the complete experience. Though he's amassed a long discography of solo records, **Silent Tongues** is the perfect Cecil snapshot. A festival recording made on a good piano live at Montreux in 1974, in its original release it was way too much music to sound great on vinyl LP – 26 minutes per side! – but the fidelity is much better on its CD reissue.

Though *Silent Tongues* is broken into five movements, it's best understood as a continuous unfolding of sections. He had long ago broken away from the idea of playing tunes, per se, although there's an untypical exception here in the form of **After All**, the Billy Strayhorn ballad included as a dedication to the recently deceased Duke Ellington, one of the pianist's heroes. Taylor has been quoted as saying that he's been playing the same song for the last thirty years, and indeed he grapples with a finite set of motifs and themes, melodic material that he's found infinite ways to vary. From the outset, the eighteen-minute **Abyss** sets the terrain – a glimpse down into the pit, with terrifying emotional torrents, careening sweeps, hammering rhythms, impossibly sudden slashes. Taylor builds tension by shifting flows of intensity, expanding and contracting rhythms like the contour of a wave. He skips up and down the keyboard, leaping from octave to octave, playing the same phrase backwards and forwards.

Crossing is built on a motif voiced as if his two hands were looking in the mirror, playing like-minded shapes. At the section's thrilling climax, the pianist settles on a high staccato repetition, using it as a call, to which he responds with lower rumbles. The music hits a plateau, shifts, resumes, shifts, ends. But, after the manhandling of the first two-thirds of the record, "After All" introduces a sweet, lyrical element – something more prevalent in Taylor's solos in recent years – that's contrasted with ominous lines and a vertiginous outburst in the middle. There are two short encores: one a return to the severity of the earlier parts, and the other the gorgeous and lush final two minutes. A tender, but firm, caress after such turbulence.

Taylor plays marathon music, with an emphasis on catharsis. He's got relentless stamina and imperturbable concentration, and when he gets warmed up, as he is the entire time on *Silent Tongues*, he's one of the most magnificent, iconoclastic virtuosos jazz has ever known.

⮌We almost chose **Nefertiti The Beautiful One Has Come**,

Revenant, 1997 [1962]

Jack Teagarden

Think Well Of Me

Verve, 1998 [rec. 1962]

Teagarden (trombone, vocals) with strings, plus Don Goldie (trumpet), probably
Bernie Leighton (piano, celeste), probably Barry Galbraith (guitar), Art Davis (bass),
Bob Brookmeyer, Russ Case, Claus Ogerman (arranger, conductor).

A quote (circa 1956) from arranger and fellow trombonist Bill Russo perfectly sums up Jack Teagarden: "It wasn't until a few years ago that I realized that Teagarden *is* the best trombonist. He has an unequalled mastery of his instrument which is evident in the simple perfection of his performance, not in sensational displays; the content of his playing illustrates a deep understanding of compositional principles – and this is the true unspoken ultimate of the jazz improviser."

Teagarden was, and remains, jazz's definitive trombone-genius. Other players (Dickie Wells, Vic Dickenson, J.J. Johnson) may have found alternative approaches, but none have left so deep an impression on jazz history as the slow-talking amicable Texan. Teagarden created for the trombone what Louis Armstrong did for the trumpet – a self-defined vocabulary combining authority, absolute musicality and style rather than stylistic mannerism. Everything he played – from what is thought to be his first solo, on Roger Wolfe Kahn's "She's A Great Great Girl!" from March 1928 – sounded exactly right. Via his trombone and irresistibly charming lazy singing, Jack Teagarden quickly became a star; first on his own, then with bandleader Paul Whiteman (1933–1938), before forming his own orchestra (1939–46) and afterwards joining Louis Armstrong's All Stars (1947–51). From then on until his death – by now a world celebrity – he led a succession of bands that increased in polished perfection as the years went by, and from 1959–62 his group included the brilliant young trumpeter Don Goldie (whose own idol was Billy Butterfield) combined exuberance and audacious creativity – which garnered both praise and occasional tight-lipped critique from less fun-loving listeners – but he was to be Teagarden's perfect partner in what is often thought to be the trombonist's most irresistible album of all, **Think Well Of Me**.

There are plenty of contenders for the accolade, but *Think Well Of Me* was certainly a stroke of recorded programming genius. Dedicated to the compositions of Willard Robison, a rural predecessor to Hoagy Carmichael, ten songs of his (plus one by Jimmy McHugh) were framed amid string arrangements by Russ Case, Bob Brookmeyer and Claus Ogerman. Their folksy quality suited Teagarden's lazy voice perfectly, and the air of nostalgic melancholy in songs like **Round My Old Deserted Farm**, **Old Folks** and the self-reproachingly funny **Country Boy Blues** touchingly matched the air of gentle fatigue which, by now, was hovering around his performance. But Teagarden was still a trombonist capable of all his old wonders, as every one of his solos demonstrates: the opening of **In A Little Waterfront Café** illustrates exactly what Russo meant, and the (all-instrumental) track **I'm Just Wild About My Mama** achieves an extraordinary profundity. On this track, as regularly elsewhere, Goldie parades his exceptional talent, climbing effortlessly with open horn to his faultless upper register in a sudden relieving move from minor to major key. Elsewhere the trumpeter is outstanding, too. His carefree opening to **T'aint So, Honey T'aint So** is as airily fresh as a country zephyr, and on **Don't Smoke In Bed** his gracious contribution is brass performance of the highest order; on the vocal return that follows, his elder leader is audibly moved. This was to be Teagarden's penultimate studio recording – its title might be his worthy epitaph.

⮱We almost chose **The Indispensable Jack Teagarden 1928–57**,

Jazz Tribune, 1992

94

Stan Tracey

Jazz Suite: Under Milk Wood

Jazzizit, 1999 (rec. 1965)

Tracey (piano), Bobby Wellins (tenor-sax), Jeff Clyne (bass), Jackie Dougan (drums).

Inspired by the radio play commemorated in the names of the eight tunes that make up the suite, **Under Milk Wood** was recorded at a time when free forms were in the ascendant. These were allied to a burgeoning musical nationalism, so that people even questioned whether Europeans had any business playing jazz, at least in a manner that reflected its American origins. More than 35 years on, acknowledged as a classic and rarely out of the catalogues, *Under Milk Wood* effortlessly proves that British jazz musicians don't have to chuck the baby out with the bath water.

Part of the generation weaned on bebop and its derivatives, Stan Tracey could not avoid differing from them to a degree because his idols were Duke Ellington and Thelonious Monk. He claims Ellington as his original inspiration, but it was the influence of Monk, enjoying a honeymoon with critics and fans after years of neglect, that stood out more, though nobody now makes the mistake of exaggerating it. Tracey hits the keys hard, loves discords and his chordal patterns move in a crabwise motion, but the details and overall approach copy Monk no more than, say, Teddy Wilson copies Earl Hines.

If Tracey was unique among pianists, Bobby Wellins also stood out from other British saxophonists, especially for his ability to use space and play within himself rather than permanently cover all options. Among the American models available at the time, Johnny Griffin's tone had a similar murky quality but that's as far as it went. The wailing, slightly off-centre sounds the Glasgow-born Wellins regularly produces have been compared to the sound of bagpipes: a few places to check these out include the theme-statement of **Under Milk Wood** itself, his improvised bridge to **Cockle Row**, the deftly timed opening bars of **Penpals** and the particularly inventive and well-proportioned solo on **No Good Boyo**.

The album's extra glow comes from the material; all pieces have stood the test of time as tunes you wish to hear again and as vehicles for self-expression. They also refuse to conform to any of the then-prevailing jazz idioms, though (again) Tracey's lineage can be drawn from the Monk echoes in parts of **Llareggub** and **AM Mayhem** and from the vaguely Ellingtonish blues theme of **I Lost My Step In Nantucket**, underpinned by a shuffle beat from Jackie Dougan. On this trio number, Tracey times everything to perfection, piling high the coruscating chords but still leaving gaps for Jeff Clyne's bass to cut through. One can spot his sheer class from bits of detail – the final piano chord of "Nantucket", for instance, or his exit from the bridge of "Penpals". Both piano and tenor keep their cool, exchanging phrases with the drums on "Cockle Row", a routine during which front-line soloists often whizz around.

Excellent as they are, the tunes have become so identified with the suite that outsiders rarely play them, though Tracey recorded a version ten years later with his then-current line-up. He must have had Wellins in mind when he wrote it, because melodies such as "No Good Boyo", and "Under Milk Wood" itself, seem tailored to that bleak tenor sound. That goes even more for **Starless And Bible Black**. A study in grim desolation as the title implies, the very slow tempo and modal backcloth recall Miles Davis's "Flamenco Sketches" – in which connection, it's worth noting that the marvellous playing by Wellins, featured almost throughout, puts one in mind more of Davis than John Coltrane.

⮑We almost chose **Solo: Trio**, Cadillac, 1997

95

Sarah Vaughan

Swingin' Easy

EmArcy, 1992 (rec. 1954–57)

Vaughan (vocals), John Malachi, Jimmy Jones (piano), Joe Benjamin, Richard Davis (bass), Roy Haynes (drums).

The voice of Vaughan was the one of wonders of jazz and popular music. Its qualities ranged from the pseudo-operatic, especially in her later period, to the earthiness that earned her nickname of "Sassy". From early on, it was applied with equal dedication to everything from trivial ditties to great standards for, like her predecessors Billie Holiday and Ella Fitzgerald, she initially left her choice of material to insensitive producers. As a result, she achieved a few hit records (the biggest was the 1958 "Broken-Hearted Melody", which she apparently grew to loathe), but later, when pop tastes had changed, she refused to make albums at all rather than record songs less appropriate to her talents.

During the period when her studio commitments allowed for both avenues of expression, she made several sessions with jazz instrumentalists including a notable set with the early Miles Davis (*In Hi-Fi*, Columbia) and one with Clifford Brown (simply titled *Sarah Vaughan*, Verve). These always revealed her fine sense of timing and her improvised variations, which had attracted the attention of Gillespie and Parker back in the 1940s and which she was forced to keep under wraps on her pop outings. A little of this did come through on orchestral projects addressing, for instance, her duets with Billy Eckstine and the songs of Irving Berlin, but what will survive longest is the small-group work that went on to influence the likes of Betty Carter.

Apart from a couple of late 1940s tracks with just a rhythm-section, the album **Swingin' Easy** is the one early album which offers Vaughan's musicality at its most exposed. Appearing with piano, bass and drums was nevertheless her normal method of working in public – any additions at all were usually strictly for the studio – and so, in the days before location recording was done with any frequency, this was an attempt to reproduce Sarah "live in the studio". (In the same year as the initial 10" album session, the same label offered a similar treatment of Dinah Washington, but she performed before a loud, invited audience which, thankfully, was not used for the Vaughan project.)

Her regular trio, in which the little-known Malachi (a former colleague from the Eckstine big-band days) replaced the temporarily indisposed Jones, is fairly self-effacing except on the famous **Shulie-A-Bop**. Here, Sarah improvises with soaring freedom over the chords of "Summertime" and announces sixteen-bar solo spots for her accompanists, the words "Roy Haynes" being punctuated by the drummer himself. There's further subtle humour in the version of **They Can't Take That Away From Me**, while **Lover Man** (one of a couple of inclusions associated with Billie Holiday) contains a wonderful melodic variation, still copied to this day by such as Oleta Adams. The tracks added for the 12" LP release (bringing in the distinctive piano of Jones and Richard Davis on bass) contain a thoughtful **Pennies From Heaven** and two uptempo romps through **I Cried For You** and the initially unreleased **Linger Awhile**.

This excellent portrait of the still-fresh-faced, innocently inventive Vaughan stands in contrast to some of her more studied later work, where the technique and the imagination are often deployed in equally daring but somewhat deliberate manner. The yet more exposed setting of just guitar and bass underlines her expertise on the 1961 *After Hours*, while an Indian summer series for the Pablo label includes the undervalued *Crazy And Mixed Up*, her self-description belied by its being her one and only self-produced album.

⮌We almost chose **After Hours**, Roulette, 1997 [1961]

96

Fats Waller

Ain't Misbehavin': 25 Greatest Hits

ASV Living Era, 1995

Waller (piano, organ, celeste, vocals), solo and with his "Rhythm", including Herman Autrey, Bill Coleman, John Hamilton, Dave Wilkins (trumpet), George Chisholm (trombone), Gene Sedric, Rudy Powell, Alfie Khan (reeds), Al Casey, James Smith, Alan Ferguson (guitar), Charles Turner, Cedric Wallace, Len Harrison (bass), Yank Porter, Slick Jones, Harry Dial Edmundo Ros (drums), Adelaide Hall (vocals), plus others.

Despite his death at only 39, almost sixty years ago, Fats Waller's musical legacy is still well remembered in jazz history for his outstanding stride-piano, catalogue of classic compositions, and sheer capacity for having fun with the music. From 1922, when he cut his first piano-rolls for QRS, Waller rapidly climbed the ladder to fame, working as everything from accompanist to piano and organ soloist, radio and recording artist and composer. By 1929 his hits (some written for the black revues *"Keep Shufflin'"* and *"Hot Chocolates"*) included **Ain't Misbehavin'**, "Black and Blue", "Sweet Savannah Sue", **Honeysuckle Rose** and **Blue Turning Grey Over You**. Then, in 1934, Waller finally signed with RCA Victor to record as bandleader under the title "Fats Waller and his Rhythm". This six-piece group's first recordings – twenty of them over three sessions in May, August and November 1934, and including "Honeysuckle Rose" from this collection – caused a sensation, sold heavily, and subsequently internationally. By the following year Waller was turning out a succession of recorded hits (all on this set too!) – including **I'm Gonna Sit Right Down And Write Myself A Letter**, **My Very Good Friend The Milkman** and **When Somebody Thinks You're Wonderful** (1935), **Until The Real Thing**

Comes Along (1936) and **Two Sleepy People** (1938). Along with these huge successes, his "Rhythm" turned out session after session of currently published popular songs which Waller treated (variously) with respect, sentiment or (regularly) irreverence.

Fats Waller was a pianist of outstanding talent who grew up among the testing society of Harlem piano masters including Luckey Roberts, Willie "The Lion" Smith and James P. Johnson, who was both tutor and mentor to his young protégé. While Waller may not have quite reached the heights of these legendary professors, his on-record solo work has lasted into history more securely than theirs, including three classics in this collection – **Handful Of Keys** (recorded at the conclusion of a 1929 record date for Eddie Condon) as well as **Viper's Drag** and the 1927 **Alligator Crawl**, both recorded in a solo session for Waller in November 1934. By this time he was a star, featured both in short "soundies" and full-length feature movies, including, of course, *Stormy Weather* (1943), which once again featured his biggest hit, "Ain't Misbehavin'".

It's featured on this set too, with Waller accompanied this time by his "Continental Rhythm", a London group featuring Dave Wilkins, Edmundo Ros and George Chisholm. Waller plays organ here as he also does on a second London date, accompanying the great Adelaide Hall on **I Can't Give You Anything But Love**, on which Hall is audibly joyful as Fats flirts with her. Other wonders include another major comedic masterpiece, **Your Feet's Too Big** (from 1939), plus **The Joint Is Jumpin'** (1937) – both of these the subject of Waller film shorts – and **Sweet And Slow**, with Rudy Powell's almost polytonal clarinet solo. Elsewhere there are more essential Waller standards (**Squeeze Me**, **Blue Turning Grey Over You** and **I've Got A Feeling I'm Falling**) as well as classic examples of Fats having fun with other people's material on **Everybody Loves My Baby**, "Two Sleepy People" and **I Ain't Got Nobody!** All of these tracks, slotted among a total of 25, make this collection a definitive first portrait of the artist kiddingly known as the "Harmful Little Armful".

➲We almost chose **Fats Waller & His Rhythm 1934–35: Lulu's Back In Town**, Giants of Jazz, 1997

97

Weather Report

Heavy Weather

Columbia, 1997 (rec. 1976)

Wayne Shorter (soprano-sax, tenor-sax), Joe Zawinul (piano, keyboards, synth), Jaco Pastorius (electric-bass, drums), Alex Acuña (drums), Manolo Badrena (percussion).

Both Wayne Shorter and Joe Zawinul were part of the Miles Davis diaspora of the late 1960s that moved on from the ground-breaking series of jazz-meets-electric-rock associated with the *Bitches Brew* sessions. If the connection of Shorter – who played in the trumpeter's quintet and wrote much of their repertoire – was more public, Zawinul composed "In A Silent Way", the tune that announced a new direction for Davis. Formerly colleagues in Maynard Ferguson's orchestra, they started Weather Report in 1971 and wound it up in 1986.

Of all the jazz-fusion outfits, Weather Report set the most stringent compositional standards: both leaders were not just gifted writers, but Zawinul in particular became totally committed to electronics as a means of enhancing and developing a group identity. While live performances followed more closely the conventions of themes and solos – to reproduce satisfactorily the wealth of detail on some pieces, they needed a studio equipped with state-of-the-art technology, and the systems available to the concert halls of the time could not cope – their finest recordings reached new levels of structured inventiveness.

Among significant points here are the first full appearance on a Weather Report album by Jaco Pastorius, wizard of the fretless electric bass, and Zawinul's **Birdland**, the track that made

Heavy Weather a bestseller. Pastorius kicks "Birdland" off before a rumbling synthesized theme takes over. The highlight appears a third of the way through, eight joyful bars that cry out for the supplementary vocal provided over the top by Zawinul and Pastorius. One of those seemingly throwaway melodies that grip the mind, it helped broaden the appeal of this relatively uncompromising fusion group: apart from selling albums, "Birdland" could hardly fail when done live.

Zawinul's delightful **A Remark You Made** was written specifically to be boomed out by Pastorius, whose broad and reverberating lines, reminiscent in many ways of Eberhard Weber, differed from those of any electric bassist operating in North America. A pretty tune of this kind fits all too readily into a smooth-jazz format, but that's not how Weather Report do things and "A Remark You Made" stays well clear of fusion glitz.

Shorter, who is featured during the piece, plays with a hard, edgy tone more common to fusion tenor players than to the way he played in the 1960s and, indeed, the balance between his two saxophones changed noticeably around this time in favour of the soprano. A big influence on those coming after, he developed an unusually pure tone, unlike those of either Bechet or Coltrane, and loves to squeeze notes like aural pear-drops that seem to hang in the air. Examples proliferate on **Harlequin**, a romantic melody typical of those Shorter writes to feature his soprano and a performance that, again, skirts the clichés of smooth jazz.

Apart from the brief duet between Alex Acuña and Manolo Badrena that constitutes **Rumba Mama**, the heaviest percussion passage occurs at the start of **Palladium**, Shorter's composition built around a repeated theme that turns ingeniously almost into church bells. Zawinul's **The Juggler** starts with the most abstract couple of minutes on the album and runs through synthesizer effects, including more chimes. On **Teen Town**, mainly a feature for his aggressively adept bass playing in both solo and ensemble, Pastorius also powers the entire piece from the drums.

➲We almost chose **Black Market**, Columbia, 1992 [1976]

98

Cassandra Wilson

Blue Light 'Til Dawn

Blue Note, 1993

Wilson (vocals), with various ensembles including Ôlu Dara (cornet), Don Byron (clarinet), Charlie Burnham (violin), Brandon Ross, Gib Wharton, Chris Whitley (guitar), Tony Cedras (accordion), Kenny Davis, Lonnie Plaxico (bass), Lance Carter (drums), Bill McLellan (drums, percussion), Cyro Baptista (percussion), Vinx (vocals, percussion).

As the vocalist identified with Steve Coleman's so-called M-Base movement that put jazz improvisation over a hip hop beat, Cassandra Wilson perhaps needed an image of her own. She gradually increased the number of standard songs on live gigs, showing much of Betty Carter's confidence in the freedom allowed her accompanying trio. But the next step was more radical, however retrogressive it may have seemed on the surface. No longer relying on keyboards and horns, she used a variety of guitars and stringed instruments. In place of jazz- or rock-derived fusions, she homed in on a more reflective interpretation of popular music, crucially bypassing the big-city blues in favour of their rural antecedents.

The first evidence on disc was **Blue Light 'Til Dawn**. Her producer, Craig Street, who picked the songs from which she made her final choice, knew that Wilson played guitar and suggested she use one to sketch ideas for the album. Guitarist Brandon Ross, who became part of her backing group, arranged five of the songs. Two of these were linked indelibly to the 1930s blues legend Robert Johnson, whose work, by comparison with the output of such postwar artists as Muddy Waters and Howlin' Wolf, had rarely been covered, let alone by women. Of the remainder, only the opening **You Don't Know What Love Is** could be considered part of the usual jazz repertory.

Wilson's voice, pitched deep and of a smoky texture but without the blues singer's raunchiness, perfectly matches her exquisitely allusive approach. If anything, she resembles a cooler version of Nina Simone, the similarities perhaps most marked when she croons over the gentle rock beat on **Tupelo Honey**. Both Johnson pieces get unusual but highly effective settings: the bluesy guitar lines from Ross, common to both, blend with accordion on **Come On In My Kitchen** and with cornet on **Hellhound On My Trail**. Featuring just Ross and Olu Dara along with voice, the latter definitely counts among the highlights, as Wilson's cloudy tones and oblique reading of the well-known lyric mesh with the interjections, gruff or lowing, from Dara's cornet.

This leads directly into **Black Crow**, the only other track to feature a horn player. The arrangement by Cyro Baptista for six percussionists plus clarinet gives Don Byron plenty of room to fill in behind and to stretch his spiky lines over the jungle-type backcloth. Wilson stays cool to even greater effect on **Children Of The Night**, where she hums to herself and puts over the song's desolate message against more percussion and against vocal interpolations by Vinx.

A songwriter from the start of her career, Wilson wrote the title tune, which sparkles in an arrangement by Charlie Burnham for his violin, percussion and the steel guitar of Gib Wharton, whose reverberations remind one of the noise Bill Frisell makes. On **Sankofa**, Wilson turns herself through overdubs into an unaccompanied choir, conjuring astonishing low notes as her chant imparts an African feel. Arguably the best is saved for the end: on a duet between voice and Chris Whitley's guitar, Wilson builds an aching intensity as she moans the lost-love lyrics to **I Can't Stand The Rain**.

Since this was recorded, the concept has developed and become somewhat heavier. The outline remains, though, securing Wilson's place among the supreme vocal stylists.

⮌We almost chose **Live**, JMT, 1991

99

Lester Young

The Jazz Giants

Verve, undated (rec. 1956)

Lester Young (tenor-sax), Roy Eldridge (trumpet), Vic Dickenson (trombone), Teddy Wilson (piano), Freddie Green (guitar), Gene Ramey (bass), Jo Jones (drums).

By the 1950s, Lester Young – the saxophone giant who first challenged the supremacy of Coleman Hawkins with a viably artistic alternative – was seen, sometimes, as a broken tenor-reed. His harmonically rooted, light-toned innovations which had spread space and light through the prewar Count Basie ensemble had been adopted (and sometimes expanded) by newer players including the phenomenal Stan Getz. And now, at times, Young – still known to all as "Prez" – seemed to be permanently overshadowed by his modern-jazz juniors. These worries, combined with sometimes unsympathetic musical company (including Norman Granz's high-powered JATP circuses in which Young's effort to conform sometimes resembled a bear dancing to a whip) took their toll, and by 1955, after heavy drinking, he wound up in Bellevue Hospital having suffered a nervous breakdown.

His recording career reflects this fact, too. Sides for Granz with Oscar Peterson show regular signs of fatigue amid reiterated splendours, and by a late date in 1958 – *Laughin' To Keep From Cryin'* with Roy Eldridge and Harry Edison – Young sounded as good as immobilized. Recording is a day-by-day business, of course, but even so **The Jazz Giants** – recorded just two years earlier – is, by any standards, a late triumph for the tired tenorist. Despite the preponderance of middle and slow tempos (four out of five selections), Young sounds, from the outset, at ease among longtime colleagues who knew what he wanted musically, and therefore how to make him sound good. Pianist Teddy Wilson, that elegant virtuoso of the swing years, had masterminded many of the dates on which Young's incomparable musical partnership with Billie Holiday had blossomed before the war. Freddy Green and Jo Jones had been blood brothers in Count Basie's orchestra at the same period and, like Wilson, understood the already disappearing art of accompaniment in jazz. Bassist Gene Ramey had taken lessons from Walter Page, Basie's bassist, early on. The front line was completed by Vic Dickenson (who had shared a year in Basie's orchestra with Young from January 1940) and the indomitable trumpeter, Roy "Little Jazz" Eldridge.

Together in the studio, this team of swing contemporaries resembled a returning "Magnificent Seven" and they demonstrate their references conclusively. Roy Eldridge (who, like Young, occasionally succumbed to the physical pressures of performance) is magnificent, arguably stealing the date with a frank and gaily stated open solo on **I Didn't Know What Time It Was**, assured statements on **This Year's Kisses** and **You Can Depend On Me**, and definitive red-hot outing on **Gigantic Blues**, punctuated by groans of concentrated effort. Dickenson's avuncular humour (full of tonal smears, sly slides and occasional bucolic explosions amid stylistic grace) is inimitable throughout, and Wilson's piano (especially on "I Didn't Know What Time It Was" and "You Can Depend On Me") is a somehow comforting affirmation of good old values. Young, audibly the elder statesman, is all over the date. He plays first and last on Arthur Schwartz's exquisite **I Guess I'll Have To Change My Plan**, plus "I Didn't Know What Time It Was" and "This Year's Kisses" (an old hit with Holiday) as well as providing a definitive final statement on "You Can Depend On Me", and tears into the album's one (very) uptempo track, "Gigantic Blues", almost as if he had never taken a solo before, returning again at the end to complete the course without running out of steam. His revived energy somehow suggests an old man rewalking old routes amid a new springtime.

⮥We almost chose **Lester Young With The Oscar Peterson Trio**, Verve, 1997 [1952]

John Zorn

Godard/Spillane

Tzadik, 1999 (rec. 1985–87)

Zorn (alto-sax, reeds, narration), Jim Staley (trombone), Anthony Coleman, David Weinstein (keyboards), Bill Frisell, Fred Frith (guitar), David Hofstra (bass, tuba), Bobby Previte (drums), Ikue Mori (drum-machine), Christian Marclay (turntables), Bob James (tapes, CDs), Carol Emanuel (harp), Luli Shioi, Wu Shao-Ying, Richard Foreman, John Lurie, Robert Quine (narration).

In the late 1970s, New York enjoyed a surge of creative underground activity: the Downtown improvising scene. A cadre of new figures – some coming from jazz and free music, many from other backgrounds like punk rock and new-classical music – began playing a highly eclectic style at little spaces in the Village, including one that would become famous, the Knitting Factory. Cast as the iconoclastic bad boy, John Zorn was central to all this activity, both as a musician-composer and as an organizer, producer and promoter.

If one of the central aspects of this Downtown scene was its omnivorous eclecticism, then Zorn's expeditions into jump-cut methodology are the movement's signal works. One of Zorn's most-discussed influences was Carl Stalling, whose compositions for Warner Brothers cartoons turned non sequitur into modus operandi. Zorn adapted the concept, but without images as anchors, thereby further emphasizing the power of genre juxtaposition. It's a textbook alienation strategy: take something familiar and make it seem new by decontextualizing it and placing it in an unfamiliar setting.

In this mode, Zorn is best known for his band Naked City, with which he gained international recognition in the late 1980s. But the jump-cut is an editing concept, something specific to the studio, and Naked City's live genre-splicing, deft as it was, could never be as fast or seamless as Zorn's actual film music (documented on several CD compilations) or two outstanding "aural cinema" pieces Zorn tracked in the legendary Radio City Studios, **Godard** and **Spillane**. They're both lengthy collages, built methodically around a central topical figure, using filing cards to organize a sequence of episodes (in *Spillane*, sixty of them). *Godard* was first issued on the small French label Nato, while *Spillane* made its debut while Zorn was signed to Nonesuch. They've been coupled now on Zorn's own label, Tzadik, in a deluxe package with garish illustrations and in-depth notes, accompanied by a six-minute bonus, **Blues Nöel**.

Godard pays homage to the French filmmaker and fellow jump-cutter. Disparate elements meet head-on in a series of shocking segues: spoken narration (in English, French, Japanese and Chinese), bits of eerie Bernard Hermann-esque soundtrack, bleating free jazz, swing, exotica, easy-listening harp, sampled vinyl, obnoxious rock, Latin soul, Peking opera, grimy noise-guitar and folksy banjo by future fret hero Bill Frisell. "There comes a time when everything has been seen," reads playwright Richard Foreman at the piece's finish. If that observation is true, then the aim is to recombine already-seen things in novel ways. Zorn's goal: a smorgasbord in sound, miraculously stitched together.

In **Spillane**, the topic more overtly governs Zorn's choice of material. John Lurie plays the part of hard-boiled detective novelist Mickey Spillane's main man, Mike Hammer. Many of the same kinds of elements flit by, but there's an overarching film-noir tone to the piece. Sound effects set a chiaroscuro stage: cars, crowds, windscreen wipers, stripper music, bloody-murder screams. For an interesting comparison, the work of video artist Abigail Child is worth seeking out; Child used many of the same musicians, and her videos use a combination of found and created sources, juxtaposed for maximum impact. With its double-barrelled irony and encyclopedic references, *Spillane* is the purest example of musical montage from the vibrant days of Downtown.

➲We almost chose **Locus Solus**, Tzadik, 1996 [1983]